Prompt Engineering: Master the Art of Asking AI

Practical Strategies & Real-World Applications

By

Dr. Rakesh Vanzara

Dr. Paresh Solanki

Dr. Devang Pandya

ISBN
Hardcase 979-8-89961-528-3
Paperback 979-8-89961-527-6

Contents

Part–2
Read Only Once Are Through Part-1 and Increased Productivity by 20%

Preface

Welcome to the forefront of human-AI interaction. In an era where artificial intelligence is rapidly reshaping our world, the ability to communicate effectively with these powerful systems is no longer a niche skill-it is a fundamental capability. Large Language Models (LLMs) like ChatGPT, Claude, Gemini, and their contemporaries possess extraordinary potential, but unlocking it requires more than simple queries. It demands the art and science of prompt engineering.

This book, Prompt Engineering: Mastering the art of asking AI, is designed to be your comprehensive guide on this exciting journey. Whether you are a developer, writer, marketer, business professional, student, or simply an AI enthusiast, our goal is to equip you with the practical strategies, advanced techniques, and real-world insights needed to move from basic interaction to true mastery in guiding AI. We believe in balancing a deep understanding of the fundamentals with hands-on, actionable methods that you can apply immediately.

Your adventure begins by dissecting the very essence of AI communication, understanding the anatomy of a powerful prompt and the core principles that drive effective interaction (Chapters 1-2). From there, you will progress rapidly, mastering advanced techniques like Chain-of-Thought reasoning, few-shot learning, and role-based prompting, learning to tailor your approach for the unique characteristics of different AI models (Chapters 3-4). We'll explore the thrilling creative frontiers, using prompts to generate art, music, and stories (Chapter 5), before diving into the pragmatic world of business, automating workflows across diverse functions like customer support, marketing, HR, and finance (Chapter 6).

Mastery, however, comes with responsibility. We navigate the crucial landscape of AI ethics and bias, equipping you to craft prompts that promote fairness and accuracy (Chapter 7), while teaching you the essential skills of measuring and iteratively improving the performance of your prompts (Chapter 8). We then gaze into the future, exploring emerging trends like self-prompting AI and multimodal interactions (Chapter 9), grounding these possibilities with real-world case studies of successful prompt engineering across industries (Chapter 10) and introducing the vital tools and communities in your Prompt Engineering Toolbox (Chapter 11) and concluding with reflections on your journey and the path ahead (Chapter 12).

Finally, we delve into advanced, enterprise-level strategies, covering sophisticated system prompting (Chapter 13), multi-model orchestration (Chapter 14), multimodal integration (Chapter 15), and domain-specific specialization (Chapter 16), and Building AI Agents (Chapter 17).

A Note on AI Collaboration in This Book

In the spirit of transparency and demonstrating the principles discussed within these pages, it's important to acknowledge that AI tools were used extensively throughout the creation of this book. Reflecting the very techniques we teach, AI assisted in various stages, including refining phrasing for clarity and conciseness, simplifying complex technical concepts, generating diverse examples and illustrative prompts, drafting initial summaries for chapters, suggesting alternative structures, and even helping to brainstorm illustration concepts based on detailed textual prompts.

This collaboration was intentional – a way to "practice what we preach" and leverage AI as a powerful partner in the writing and content generation process. However, it is crucial to emphasize that every piece of AI-generated or AI-assisted content underwent rigorous review, editing, fact-checking, and final approval by the human author. The insights, analyses, strategic recommendations, structure, and ultimate accuracy of this work remain entirely the author's responsibility. We believe this transparent approach models the ethical and effective human-AI partnership that lies at the heart of prompt engineering.

Embarking on the path to mastering prompt engineering is an investment in your future relevance and capability. The skills you acquire will empower you to innovate, create, and solve problems in ways previously unimaginable. We are thrilled you are taking this journey with us. The world of AI is dynamic and constantly evolving; stay curious, keep experimenting, and embrace the power of effective communication. The future of human-AI partnership is waiting to be written, and you now hold the pen-or rather, the prompt.

PART–1

Welcome to Journey of Improving Productivity

CHAPTER 1

The Fundamentals of Prompt Engineering

1.1   Introduction to Prompt Engineering

Artificial Intelligence (AI) has rapidly evolved in recent years, with large language models (LLMs) like **ChatGPT, Claude, Gemini, and LLaMA** leading the way in transforming human-machine interaction. These models can generate text, answer complex queries, assist in creative writing, and even develop code. However, their effectiveness depends on **how well they are prompted**.

Prompt Engineering is the **art and science of crafting effective inputs (prompts) to guide AI models** toward generating precise, relevant, and high-quality responses. A well-structured prompt can significantly enhance the **accuracy, clarity, and creativity** of AI-generated outputs.

This chapter lays the groundwork for understanding prompt engineering, covering its importance, core principles, and the different types of prompts used in AI interactions.

1.2   What is a Prompt?

A **prompt** is the input provided to an AI model to elicit a desired response. It can be as simple as a question or as complex as a structured instruction with constraints.

Example 1: Basic vs. Structured Prompt

📝 **Basic Prompt:**

"Explain machine learning."

📝 Structured Prompt:

"Explain machine learning in simple terms, as if you are teaching a 10-year-old. Use a real-world analogy."

💡 Why does this matter?

The second prompt provides context and a target audience, helping the AI model tailor its response accordingly.

1.3   Understanding AI Language Models (LLMs)

To effectively engineer prompts, it's essential to understand **how AI language models work**. Artificial Intelligence has transformed how we interact with technology, with large language models (LLMs) like ChatGPT, Claude, Gemini, and LLaMA leading this revolution. These sophisticated AI systems can generate human-like text, solve complex problems, create content, and write code. However, their effectiveness fundamentally depends on the quality of prompts they receive.

How AI Models Interpret Prompts

Most AI language models use **Natural Language Processing (NLP)** techniques to analyze input text and generate human-like responses. These models predict the most likely **next word or phrase** based on the context of the prompt.

Key Factors Influencing AI Responses:

1. **Prompt Clarity:** The clearer the instruction, the better the response.
2. **Context Length:** More context improves the quality of generated outputs.
3. **Temperature Settings:** Adjusting randomness in AI responses (higher values = more creative, lower values = more deterministic).

4. **Training Data:** The AI model's knowledge is based on its training data, affecting response accuracy.

💡 **Example of Model Behavior:**

- Asking **"What is AI?"** will give a generic response.
- Asking **"Explain AI in three bullet points, with examples."** leads to a structured and useful response.

💡 **Understanding the AI Communication Paradigm:** At its core, prompt engineering is about effective communication with AI systems. Unlike human conversation, which relies on shared context and implicit understanding, AI communication requires explicit instruction and careful framing. The AI model doesn't "know" what you want unless you tell it clearly. Consider the cognitive framework of modern AI models:

- ✓ They process text as statistical patterns rather than with human-like understanding
- ✓ They have no inherent goals or intentions beyond responding to your input
- ✓ They lack common sense unless it's explicitly encoded in your prompt
- ✓ They don't remember previous interactions unless you include that context

This fundamental difference between human and AI cognition means that successful prompting requires a different communication approach than you might use with humans.

The Evolution of Prompt Complexity: The evolution of prompt engineering reflects the increasing sophistication of AI models:

First Generation (2020-2021): Simple question-answer formats

- Example: "What is artificial intelligence?"
- Limitations: Generic responses, lack of specificity

Second Generation (2021-2022): Instruction-based prompting

- Example: "Explain artificial intelligence in simple terms."
- Improvements: More directed responses, better clarity

Third Generation (2022-2023): Role and context-based prompting

- Example: "You are an AI expert teaching a beginner. Explain artificial intelligence using simple analogies."
- Advancements: Tailored responses, improved relevance, better tone control

Fourth Generation (2023-Present): Multi-step, reasoning-focused prompting

- Example: "You are an AI expert teaching a beginner. First, explain what artificial intelligence is using a simple analogy. Then, describe three real-world applications. Finally, address one common misconception about AI."
- Benefits: Complex reasoning, structured outputs, higher quality responses

This progression demonstrates how prompt engineering has evolved from simple queries to sophisticated, multi-part instructions that guide AI through complex reasoning processes.

1.4   Types of Prompts

1. Standard Prompts (Basic Queries)

These are simple questions or statements that ask for information.

📝 **Example:**

"What is quantum computing?"

📌 **Use Case:** Quick factual answers.

2. Instruction-Based Prompts

These provide specific instructions for AI to follow.

📝 **Example:**

"Write a 200-word summary on blockchain technology for beginners."

📌 **Use Case:** Writing tasks, summarization, explanation requests.

3. Contextual Prompts

These provide background information or constraints to **narrow AI responses**.

📝 **Example:**

"Explain cloud computing in 5 bullet points, focusing on its benefits for startups."

📌 **Use Case:** Precise explanations tailored to a specific need.

4. Chain-of-Thought (CoT) Prompts

These prompt the AI to **think step-by-step**, leading to better logical reasoning.

📝 **Example:**

"If a train departs at 9 AM and travels at 60 km/h for 3 hours, at what time does it reach its destination? Explain step-by-step."

📌 **Use Case:** Problem-solving, math calculations, reasoning tasks.

📌 **Benefits:** More accurate results for complex problems

5. Role-Based Prompts

Here, AI is assigned a role to guide its response style.

📝 **Example:**

"You are a cybersecurity expert. Explain phishing attacks and how to prevent them."

📌 **Use Case:** Simulating experts, creative storytelling, generating role-specific answers.

1.5   The Evolution of Prompt Engineering

Prompt engineering has evolved from simple commands to **highly structured** and **complex** instructions.

Era	Prompt Style	AI Model Used
Early AI (Pre-2020)	Basic text commands	GPT-2, BERT
AI Boom (2020-2022)	Structured prompts	GPT-3, T5
Present (2023-2025)	Advanced, role-based, multi-turn prompts	GPT-4, Claude, Gemini, LLaMA

💡 **Key Takeaway:** The field is rapidly advancing, and those who master **structured prompting** will get the most value from AI models.

1.6   Case Study: Good vs. Bad Prompts in Action

To illustrate the importance of well-crafted prompts, let's compare **a bad prompt vs. a well-optimized prompt** for the same task.

Example: AI-Generated Email Response

❌ **Bad Prompt:**

"Write an email."

☑ **Good Prompt:**

"Write a professional email to a client apologizing for a delayed shipment, offering a discount for future purchases."

📌 **Result:** The second prompt ensures **better AI output** by specifying the **tone, audience, and context**.

1.7   The Prompt Engineering Mindset

Successful prompt engineers adopt a particular mindset:

1. Precision: Being exact about what you want

- Specify format, length, tone, and audience
- Define parameters clearly (e.g., "Write a 300-word explanation...")

2. Iteration: Refining prompts based on results

- Test different approaches and analyse responses
- Make incremental improvements based on feedback

3. Experimentation: Testing different approaches

- Try various prompt structures and techniques
- Compare results across different models

4. Systems Thinking: Understanding how the AI processes information

- Consider the model's training data and limitations
- Recognize patterns in how the AI responds to different inputs

5. User Empathy: Considering the end user's needs

- Tailor prompts to produce outputs that serve specific purposes
- Consider the context in which the AI response will be used

This mindset helps navigate the sometimes-counterintuitive nature of AI interaction. For instance, being more verbose is often better than being concise, contrary to human communication best practices.

Practical Exercise: Developing Your First Structured Prompt

Let's transform a basic prompt into a more effective one:

Basic Prompt: "Tell me about climate change."

Improved Prompt: "You are an **environmental scientist** explaining climate change to a **high school student.** In **300 words**, explain what climate change is, its primary **causes**, three major **consequences**, and two **actions** individuals can take to help. Use **simple language** and include one compelling **statistic.**"

Analysis of Improvement:

- Added role context (environmental scientist)
- Specified audience (high school student)
- Set clear parameters (300 words)
- Outlined specific content requirements (definition, causes, consequences, actions)
- Requested specific elements (simple language, statistics)

This structured approach dramatically improves the likelihood of receiving a useful, targeted response from the AI.

1.8   Practical Exercise: Writing Your First Prompt

Try this **hands-on exercise** to improve your prompting skills!

Task: Rewrite the following generic prompt into a structured, specific, and role-based prompt.

- *Generic Prompt:* "Explain digital marketing."
- *Your Improved Prompt:* 🖋 (Make it more detailed!)

📌 **Hint:** Add a target audience (beginners? experts?), a format (bullet points? essay?), or a goal (explain benefits? give examples?).

1.9   Summary & Key Takeaways

- ✓ **Prompt Engineering** is essential for optimizing AI responses.
- ✓ Well-crafted prompts improve accuracy, clarity, and relevance.

- ✓ AI models interpret prompts based on **clarity, context, and structure**.
- ✓ Different types of prompts (basic, instruction-based, role-based) serve different purposes.
- ✓ **Practice** is key to mastering prompt engineering: **refine, test, and iterate!**

🚀 What's Next?

Now that you understand the **fundamentals**, the next chapter will explore **how to build highly effective prompts**, diving into **best practices, common mistakes, and optimization techniques**.

Congratulations on Completing chapter 1, Happy prompting and we are sure you will be 30% more productive than earlier version of yourself, once you complete the Book!

CHAPTER 2

Anatomy of a Powerful Prompt

2.1 Introduction

A well-structured prompt is the key to **getting precise, relevant, and high-quality responses from AI models**. Whether you're generating text, writing code, or asking for creative input, the structure of your prompt determines the **effectiveness and accuracy** of AI's response.

This chapter breaks down the **core components of a powerful prompt**, provides **best practices**, and explains **common mistakes to avoid**. You'll also find **real-world examples** and **interactive exercises** to sharpen your skills.

2.2 The Core Structure of an Effective Prompt

A powerful prompt is **clear, specific, and structured**. The following **four key elements** contribute to a well-engineered prompt:

1. Context (Background Information)

Provides **relevant details** to help AI understand the request.

📌 **Example:**

Instead of saying:

✖ *"Write about climate change."*

Say:

☑ *"Write a 300-word summary explaining climate change and its impact on rising sea levels, using simple language for a 12-year-old student."*

Why?

- The AI understands the target audience.
- The word limit ensures conciseness.
- The focus on rising sea levels narrows the scope.

2. Instruction (What AI Should Do)

Clearly defines the task the AI should perform.

📌 **Example:**

Instead of saying:

✖ *"Tell me about the stock market."*

Say:

☑ *"Explain the stock market in five bullet points, including its purpose, key players, and how beginners can start investing."*

Why?

- The **format (bullet points)** makes the response more structured.
- It guides AI to focus on key areas.

3. Output Format (How the Response Should Be Structured)

Specify whether you want the response in **paragraphs, bullet points, tables, or code snippets.**

📌 **Example:**

Instead of saying:

✖ *"List top AI companies."*

Say:

☑ *"Create a table of the top five AI companies, including their founding year, CEO, and key AI innovations."*

📌 **Expected Output:**

Company	Founding Year	CEO	Key Innovation
OpenAI	2015	Sam Altman	GPT-4, DALL·E
DeepMind	2010	Demis Hassabis	AlphaFold, AlphaGo

Why?

- A **table format** makes it easier to read.
- AI is guided on what details to include.

4. Constraints (Limitations or Preferences)

If you need a specific **tone, style, word limit, or exclusions**, mention them explicitly.

📌 **Example:**

Instead of saying:

✗ *"Write about electric cars."*

Say:

✅ *"Write a persuasive 200-word article about the environmental benefits of electric cars, avoiding any technical jargon."*

Why?

- The **tone** is set (persuasive).
- The **length** is defined (200 words).
- **Unwanted content** is excluded (no jargon).

2.3   Common Mistakes in Prompt Engineering

Here are some **mistakes to avoid** when crafting AI prompts:

✗ 1. Vague or Generic Prompts

Bad Prompt: *"Tell me about AI."*

✅ **Fix:** *"Explain AI in 200 words, focusing on its impact on healthcare and education."*

✗ 2. Asking Too Many Things in One Prompt

Bad Prompt: *"Explain machine learning, give me a Python code example, and summarize its history."*

✅ **Fix:** Break it into separate prompts or structure it step-by-step:

"Explain machine learning in 3 bullet points. Then provide a simple Python code example. Finally, give a brief history in two sentences."

✗ 3. Ignoring Output Format

Bad Prompt: *"List famous entrepreneurs."*

✅ **Fix:** *"Create a numbered list of 5 famous entrepreneurs, their companies, and one major contribution of each."*

2.4   The Psychology of AI Prompting

Understanding how AI "thinks" helps create more effective prompts:

Priming Effects: The first part of your prompt heavily influences the AI's approach to the entire task. Starting with "Write a balanced analysis..." versus "Write a critique..." will yield dramatically different results.

Anchoring: Providing examples or references "anchors" the AI's response style. This is why few-shot prompting (providing examples) is so effective.

Framing: How you frame a request affects the response quality. "Write about climate change" versus "Explain the scientific consensus on climate change" produces very different outputs.

Recency Bias: AI models tend to focus more on the latter parts of your prompt. Place the most important instructions toward the end of your prompt for greater emphasis.

Consistency Principle: AI tries to maintain consistency with the tone, style, and approach established early in the prompt. Setting the right tone from the beginning helps maintain it throughout.

Advanced Context Setting

Context is perhaps the most powerful yet underutilized aspect of prompt engineering:

Temporal Context: Specifying period or recency

- "Explain cloud computing as understood in 2025" versus "Explain cloud computing as it was in 2010"
- Benefits: Ensures information is appropriate for the relevant time

Expertise Context: Setting the knowledge level

- "Explain quantum computing to a scholar of physics PhD" versus "Explain quantum computing to a 10-year-old"
- Benefits: Tailors explanation complexity to the audience

Cultural Context: Establishing cultural reference points

- "Explain American football to an American" versus "Explain American football to someone from India who only knows cricket"
- Benefits: Makes explanations more relevant and understandable

Situational Context: Defining the scenario

- "Write a product description for a luxury watch for a print magazine" versus "Write a product description for a luxury watch for an Instagram post"
- Benefits: Adapts content to the medium and situation

Emotional Context: Setting the emotional tone

- "Write a motivational speech for a team that just lost an important competition" versus "Write a celebratory speech for a team that just won a championship"
- Benefits: Ensures appropriate emotional resonance

Crafting Output Format Instructions

The format of AI responses can be precisely controlled:

Structural Formats:

- Paragraphs: "Write a three-paragraph explanation..."
- Lists: "Provide a numbered list of 5 key points..."
- Tables: "Create a comparison table with 3 columns..."
- Outlines: "Generate a hierarchical outline with main points and sub-points..."
- Q&A Format: "Present the information as 5 common questions with detailed answers..."

Stylistic Formats:

- Tone: "Write in a professional/casual/humorous tone..."
- Voice: "Write in first person from the perspective of..."
- Length: "Keep each point to under 30 words..."
- Complexity: "Use language appropriate for a 9th-grade reading level..."
- Formality: "Use formal academic language with proper citations..."

Visual Formatting:

- Headings: "Use clear headings and subheadings to organize the content..."
- Emphasis: "Bold key terms and italicize examples..."
- Spacing: "Separate each section with a clear break..."
- Symbols: "Use bullet points (–) for lists and arrows (→) for cause-effect relationships..."

2.5 Real-World Examples of Effective Prompting

Example 1: Blog Post Generation

✘ **Bad Prompt:** *"Write about the future of AI."*

✔ **Better Prompt:** *"Write a 500-word blog post about the future of AI, focusing on automation, job markets, and ethical challenges. Use a professional and engaging tone."*

Example 2: AI for Coding Assistance

✘ **Bad Prompt:** *"Give me Python code for data analysis."*

✔ **Better Prompt:** *"Write a Python script that reads a CSV file and calculates the average sales per month. Use Pandas and Matplotlib for visualization."*

Example 3: AI-Generated Storytelling

✘ **Bad Prompt:** *"Tell me a story."*

✔ **Better Prompt:** *"Write a 300-word science fiction story about an astronaut who lands on a mysterious planet and discovers a new intelligent species. The story should have a suspenseful tone."*

Example 4: Creating a document/report

✘ **Bad Prompt:** *"Write documentation for a REST API."*

✅ **Better Prompt:** "You are a senior technical writer creating documentation for a new REST API. Create comprehensive API documentation that includes:

1. An introduction explaining RESTful principles (100 words)
2. Authentication methods (focus on OAuth 2.0 and API keys)
3. Request/response formats with JSON examples
4. Endpoint documentation for GET, POST, PUT, and DELETE operations
5. Error handling with standard HTTP status codes
6. Rate limiting information
7. Code examples in Python and JavaScript

Format the documentation with clear headings, code blocks for examples, and tables for endpoint parameters. Use a professional but accessible tone suitable for developers with intermediate experience."

This prompt provides comprehensive guidance on content, structure, format, and tone, resulting in documentation that meets professional standards.

2.6   Practical Exercises: Test Your Prompting Skills!

Try **improving these prompts** by making them **clearer, more specific, and structured**:

Weak Prompt:

"Write about space exploration."

✏️ **Your Improved Prompt:** _________________

Weak Prompt:

"Give me marketing tips."

✏️ **Your Improved Prompt:** _________________

Weak Prompt:

"Tell me about famous scientists."

🖊 **Your Improved Prompt:** ___________________

2.7   Summary & Key Takeaways

✔ **A powerful prompt has four key elements:**

- **Context** (What is the background information?)
- **Instruction** (What should AI do?)
- **Output Format** (How should the response be structured?)
- **Constraints** (What should AI include or avoid?)

✔ **Best practices:**

- Be **specific** about the task.
- Structure the **output format** clearly.
- Use **constraints** to refine responses.
- Avoid **vague** or **overly broad** questions.

✔ **Mastering prompt engineering** helps in AI-powered writing, automation, coding, and more!

🚀 **What's Next?**

Now that you understand **how to craft powerful prompts**, the next chapter will take things further with **Advanced Prompting Techniques** like:

✔ **Chain-of-Thought (CoT) Prompting** for logical reasoning.

✔ **Role-Based Prompting** to simulate experts.

✔ **Zero-Shot, One-Shot, and Few-Shot Learning** in AI models.

✔ **Self-Consistency & Multi-Turn Prompts** for better outputs.

Answer to exercise in section 2.5 *("We never let go of our brilliant students—because greatness deserves a standing ovation, not a goodbye.")*

Improved Version: "As a NASA scientist, write an engaging 500-word article about recent Mars exploration missions for a science magazine. Include three major discoveries from the past five years, current challenges, and future mission plans. Use an informative yet accessible tone suitable for high school students with an interest in astronomy."

Improved Version: "You are a digital marketing expert advising a small e-commerce business selling handmade jewellery. Provide 7 actionable social media marketing strategies to increase their online visibility and sales. For each strategy, include: a brief explanation, implementation steps, expected results, and a real-world example. Format as a numbered list with clear headings and keep each strategy description under 100 words."

Improved Version: "Create profiles of 5 influential female scientists from different fields and time periods who made groundbreaking discoveries but received less recognition than their male counterparts. For each scientist, include: name, time period, field of study, major contributions, challenges faced due to gender bias, and their lasting impact on science. Format as a table with these categories as columns, followed by a 150-word paragraph explaining the historical context of gender discrimination in scientific fields."

CHAPTER 3

Advanced Prompt Engineering Techniques

3.1   Introduction

Now that we've covered the fundamentals of prompt engineering, it's time to explore **advanced techniques** that can significantly improve the quality of AI-generated responses.

AI models like **GPT-4, Claude, Gemini, and LLaMA** can generate better results when given **structured, multi-step prompts** that guide them logically. Advanced techniques like **Chain-of-Thought (CoT) prompting, role-based prompts, and few-shot learning** help fine-tune responses for greater accuracy, depth, and usability.

This chapter explores these **cutting-edge prompting strategies**, complete with **real-world examples and exercises** to apply them effectively.

3.2   Zero-Shot, One-Shot, and Few-Shot Learning

AI models respond differently depending on how much **guidance or context** is provided.

1. Zero-Shot Prompting

With zero-shot learning, the AI receives a **direct prompt without examples**, relying on its pre-trained knowledge.

📌 **Example:**

 **Prompt:** *"Explain blockchain technology in one paragraph."*

📝 **AI Response:** *"Blockchain is a decentralized digital ledger that records transactions securely. It eliminates intermediaries by using cryptographic techniques, ensuring transparency and security in finance, supply chains, and other industries."*

✅ **When to Use:**

- When you need a **quick answer** without requiring examples.
- For **general knowledge queries**.

2. One-Shot Prompting

Here, you provide **one example** before asking AI to generate a response.

📌 **Example:**

📝 **Prompt:**

"Here's how to write a tweet about AI in a witty tone: 'AI is like a toddler—sometimes brilliant, sometimes nonsensical, but always learning.' Now, write a tweet about quantum computing in the same tone."

📌 **AI Response:**

"Quantum computing is like a cat in a box—both solving problems and confusing scientists at the same time!"

✅ **When to Use:**

- When AI **needs a reference** for tone, style, or structure.
- For **consistent writing output**.

3. Few-Shot Prompting

Here, you provide **multiple examples** to refine AI's response.

📌 **Example:**

📝 **Prompt:**

"Here are two examples of concise book summaries:

1. *'The Great Gatsby is a novel about wealth, love, and the American Dream in the 1920s.'*
2. *'1984 explores a dystopian society where surveillance and government control dominate.'*

Now, summarize 'Pride and Prejudice' in one sentence."

📌 AI Response:

"Pride and Prejudice is a classic novel about love, class, and personal growth set in Regency-era England."

✅ When to Use:

- When AI needs **stronger context** for structured responses.
- For **creative and technical writing tasks**.

3.3 Chain-of-Thought (CoT) Prompting: Getting AI to Think Step-by-Step

Why It Works

Most AI models respond better when **thinking in steps**, instead of jumping to a direct answer.

📌 Example: Basic vs. Chain-of-Thought Prompt

✖ Bad Prompt:

"What is 17 × 23?"

📌 AI Response:

"391." (Correct but lacks reasoning)

✅ Good Prompt (Chain-of-Thought Prompting):

"Break down the multiplication of 17 × 23 step by step before giving the final answer."

📌 **AI Response:**

"Step 1: Break it down → (17 × 20) + (17 × 3)

Step 2: Calculate → (340) + (51) = 391

Final Answer: 391."

✅ **When to Use:**

- When dealing with **math, logic, or reasoning tasks**.
- When you want **AI to explain its thought process**.

3.4 Role-Based Prompting: Making AI Act as an Expert

You can **assign AI a role** to generate more specialized responses.

📌 **Example 1: AI as a Cybersecurity Expert**

📝 **Prompt:**

"You are a cybersecurity expert. Explain phishing attacks and how companies can prevent them."

📌 **AI Response:**

"Phishing attacks involve deceptive emails that trick users into revealing sensitive information. Companies can prevent them by using email filtering, multi-factor authentication, and employee training."

📌 **Example 2: AI as a Career Advisor**

📝 **Prompt:**

"You are a career coach. A 25-year-old software engineer wants to transition into AI and machine learning. Provide a 3-step plan."

📌 **AI Response:**

1. Learn Python and fundamental AI concepts.
2. Take online courses in ML (e.g., Coursera, Udacity).
3. Build ML projects and contribute to GitHub.

☑️ **When to Use:**

- When you need **expert-like responses**.
- For **industry-specific AI outputs**.

3.5   Multi-Turn Prompting: Creating AI Conversations

You can **extend AI interactions over multiple turns** by structuring them as ongoing discussions.

📌 **Example: AI Tutoring Session**

📝 **Prompt (Turn 1):**

"Explain Newton's laws of motion in simple terms."

📌 **AI Response (Turn 1):**

"Newton's first law states that objects in motion stay in motion unless acted upon by an external force..."

📝 **Prompt (Turn 2):**

"Great! Now, can you provide a real-world example of the first law?"

📌 **AI Response (Turn 2):**

"Yes! When a car suddenly stops, passengers lurch forward due to inertia."

☑️ **When to Use:**

- For **AI-driven tutoring, customer service, or storytelling**.
- When creating **multi-step responses**.

3.6   Real-World Applications of Advanced Prompting

📌 **Marketing & Content Creation**

- **Role-based prompting** for brand voices.
- **Few-shot prompting** for ad campaign consistency.

📌 **AI-Powered Coding**

- **Chain-of-Thought prompting** for debugging.
- **Multi-turn prompting** for step-by-step code explanations.

📌 **Healthcare & Legal AI**

- **Zero-shot prompting** for medical diagnoses.
- **Role-based prompting** for AI-generated legal advice.

3.7 Hands-On Exercises: Try These Prompts!

✏️ **Exercise 1:**

- Rewrite this **basic** prompt using **Chain-of-Thought prompting**:
- ✖ *"Solve 256 ÷ 4."*
- ☑ **Your Improved Prompt:** ______________

✏️ **Exercise 2:**

- Use **Role-Based prompting** for this scenario:
- ✖ *"Tell me about stock investments."*
- ☑ **Your Improved Prompt:** ______________

✏️ **Exercise 3:**

- Improve this **zero-shot prompt** by using **few-shot prompting**:
- ✖ *"Write a funny tweet about AI."*
- ☑ **Your Improved Prompt:** ______________

3.8 Summary & Key Takeaways

✔ **Zero-shot, One-shot, and Few-shot learning** control how AI generates responses.

✔ **Chain-of-Thought prompting** improves reasoning and logic.

✔ **Role-based prompting** makes AI act like an expert.

✔ **Multi-turn prompting** creates dynamic AI interactions.

✔ **Practice these techniques** to refine AI responses for different industries!

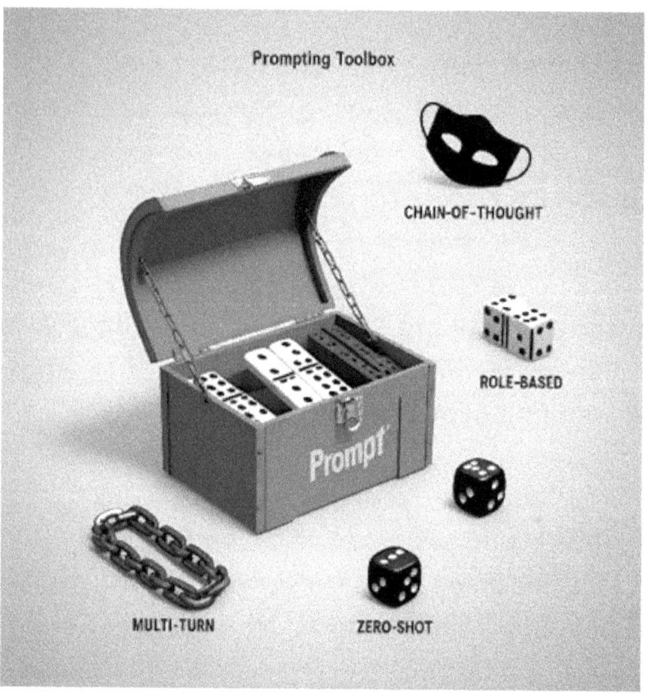

Figure 3.1: Prompting Toolbox

🚀 What's Next?

Now that you've learned **advanced prompting strategies**, the next chapter will focus on **Optimizing Prompts for Different AI Models**, where we will explore:

✔ How GPT-4, Claude, Gemini, and LLaMA interpret prompts differently.

✔ Tuning prompts for **better efficiency and relevance**.

✔ **Industry-specific prompt customization.**

As promised in chapter 2, solution to exercise:

Exercise-1: Let's solve 256 ÷ 4 step by step. First, think about how many times 4 fits into 256. You can break it down by seeing how many times 4 goes into 25, and then into 6. Show your reasoning at each step before giving the final answer.

Exercise-2: You are a seasoned financial advisor with 20 years of experience in the stock market. Explain stock investments to a beginner who has never invested before. Keep it simple, informative, and include examples of common strategies.

Exercise-3: Go to ChatGPT or Gemini and put the question, you will get the solution. *(Can't just stay theoretical—it needs doing)*

CHAPTER 4

Optimizing Prompts for Different AI Models

4.1 Introduction

Each AI model interprets prompts differently. While OpenAI's **GPT-4** might excel at detailed explanations, **Claude** (Anthropic) may prioritize safety and reasoning, and **Gemini** (Google DeepMind) could focus on factual accuracy.

To **maximize efficiency and accuracy**, prompt engineers need to **customize prompts** based on the model's architecture, strengths, and limitations.

This chapter explores how to **optimize prompts for different AI models**, including **GPT-4, Claude, Gemini, and LLaMA**, and provides best practices for fine-tuning outputs.

4.2 Understanding AI Model Differences

Model	Strengths	Limitations	Best Use Cases
GPT-4 (OpenAI)	Detailed responses, creative writing, coding	May over-elaborate, can generate incorrect facts	Essays, storytelling, customer support
Claude (Anthropic)	Ethical and safe responses, logical reasoning	Struggles with highly technical tasks	Legal, compliance, education

Model	Strengths	Limitations	Best Use Cases
Gemini (Google DeepMind)	Fast responses, real-time data integration	Less conversational depth than GPT	Search-based queries, fact-checking
LLaMA (Meta AI)	Lightweight, customizable for research	Requires fine-tuning for best performance	Research, academic AI, private models

4.3   Model-Specific Prompt Optimization Techniques

1. Optimizing Prompts for GPT-4

📌 **Strengths:** Creativity, long-form content, coding.

📌 **Best Practices:**

- Use **structured prompts** to prevent overly verbose answers.
- Utilize **role-based prompts** for technical or creative tasks.
- Include **constraints** like word limits, response formats.

📌 **Example Prompt (Optimized for GPT-4):**

"You are a software engineer. Write a concise Python function to calculate the Fibonacci sequence, including comments. Keep it under 10 lines of code."

✅ **Why It Works:**

- Assigns a **role** (software engineer).
- Limits the **code length** (10 lines).
- Includes **comments for clarity**.

2. Optimizing Prompts for Claude

📌 **Strengths:** Ethical responses, critical thinking, structured reasoning.

📌 **Best Practices:**

- Use **Chain-of-Thought (CoT) prompting** to enhance reasoning.
- Request **step-by-step explanations** for logical tasks.
- Use **ethical constraints** to ensure compliance.

📌 **Example Prompt (Optimized for Claude):**

"You are a legal expert. Explain the impact of GDPR on data privacy compliance in European businesses, using a step-by-step approach."

✅ **Why It Works:**

- Assigns an **expert role** (legal expert).
- Requests a **structured, step-by-step explanation**.
- Aligns with Claude's strength in **reasoning and compliance**.

3. Optimizing Prompts for Gemini

📌 **Strengths:** Real-time web search, accurate factual responses.

📌 **Best Practices:**

- Ask for **recent data sources** when necessary.
- Use **direct, fact-based questions** for efficiency.
- Request **comparisons** for better insights.

📌 **Example Prompt (Optimized for Gemini):**

"Compare the latest AI regulations in the US, EU, and China as of 2025. Provide key differences in a table format."

✅ **Why It Works:**

- Requests **real-time, fact-based comparisons**.
- Uses a **specific timeframe (2025)**.
- Asks for a **structured output (table format)**.

4. Optimizing Prompts for LLaMA

📌 **Strengths:** Open-source, customizable for academic and research purposes.

📌 **Best Practices:**

- Use **precise academic phrasing** for research-based tasks.
- Request **technical breakdowns** for AI-related queries.
- Leverage **fine-tuning capabilities** for domain-specific knowledge.

📌 **Example Prompt (Optimized for LLaMA):**

"Provide an academic literature review on the latest advancements in Transformer-based neural networks. Include references to key papers published after 2022."

✅ **Why It Works:**

- Uses an **academic-style prompt**.
- Asks for **recent research papers**.
- Aligns with **LLaMA's strength in research-based AI**.

4.4   Industry-Specific Prompt Optimization

Depending on the **industry or task**, prompts should be customized to suit different **AI models and applications**.

Industry	Best AI Model	Optimized Prompt Strategy
Finance	Claude, Gemini	Fact-based reports, compliance-based prompts
Healthcare	GPT-4, Gemini	Detailed explanations, medical research summaries
Marketing	GPT-4	Creative ad copy, storytelling prompts
Legal	Claude	Compliance-based reasoning, ethical AI use
Software Dev	GPT-4, LLaMA	Code generation, debugging prompts

📌 **Example for Finance:**

📝 **Optimized Prompt for Claude/Gemini:**

"Analyze the 2025 global stock market trends, focusing on AI-driven fintech innovations. Provide insights in a risk assessment format."

✅ **Why It Works:**

- Requests **real-time financial trends**.
- Specifies **AI-driven fintech focus**.
- Aligns with **Claude & Gemini's strength in fact-based analysis**.

📌 **Healthcare**

🎯 *Medical innovation summaries with regulatory context*

🧠 **Prompt:**

"Summarize recent FDA-approved AI-assisted diagnostic tools for oncology. Highlight clinical outcomes, risk factors, and compliance notes."

🤘 **Best For:** Claude, ChatGPT-4

✅ **Why:**

- Claude's strength in long-context summarization.
- GPT-4 adds nuanced understanding of medical language.
- Strong for compliance-heavy industries.

📌 **Education**

🎯 *Curriculum design with tech integration*

🧠 **Prompt:** *"Create a high school STEM curriculum that incorporates AI tools like ChatGPT, Google Colab, and simulations. Include learning outcomes, assessment methods, and engagement tips."*

🤘 **Best For: ChatGPT-4, Gemini**

✅ **Why:**

- GPT-4 is strong in lesson planning, creativity, and pedagogy.
- Gemini complements with integration of Google-based tools.

📌 **Marketing**

🎯 *Content strategy for specific audience*

🧠 **Prompt:** *"Draft a Q2 digital marketing strategy for a SaaS startup targeting Gen Z entrepreneurs. Include suggested platforms, voice/tone guidelines, and KPI benchmarks."*

🤘 **Best For: ChatGPT-4, Claude**

✅ **Why:**

- ChatGPT excels in tone, platform strategy, and engagement.
- Claude is great for structured business documentation.

📌 **Legal**

🎯 *Policy draft with contextual analysis*

🧠 **Prompt:** *"Draft a data privacy policy for a fintech app operating in the US and EU, considering GDPR, CCPA, and current case law. Include clauses with justifications."*

🤘 **Best For: Claude, ChatGPT-4**

✅ **Why:**

- Claude shines with legal logic chains and long documents.
- GPT-4 brings contextual nuance and clarity in explanation.

📌 **Human Resources**

🎯 *Inclusive job description crafting*

🧠 **Prompt:** *"Write an inclusive and engaging job description for a remote senior software engineer role. Highlight DEI values, flexibility, and career growth."*

👾 **Best For: ChatGPT-4**

✅ **Why:**

- GPT-4's tone control, diversity language, and format adaptation are ideal here.

📌 **Product Development**

🎯 *Feature analysis with user story structure*

🧠 **Prompt:** *"Propose three new AI-powered features for a mobile banking app, using user stories (As a user, I want...). Include business value and tech feasibility."*

👾 **Best For: ChatGPT-4, Gemini**

✅ **Why:**

- GPT-4 handles user-centric design well.
- Gemini connects well with Google-native mobile dev workflows.

📌 **Research / Academia**

🎯 *Literature review assistant*

🧠 **Prompt:** *"Provide a literature review summary on quantum computing applications in cryptography since 2020. Focus on key breakthroughs, authors, and citations."*

👾 **Best For: Claude (context length), ChatGPT-4 (citation mapping)**

✅ **Why:**

- Claude handles long documents and threading ideas.
- GPT-4 provides crisp academic summaries with style.

📌 **Manufacturing / Supply Chain**

🎯 *Optimization strategy for logistics*

🧠 **Prompt:** *"Analyze a hypothetical supply chain for an electronics company and suggest optimizations using predictive AI tools. Present in SWOT format."*

👹 **Best For: Gemini, ChatGPT-4**

✅ **Why:**

- Gemini excels in data logic and operational flow.
- GPT-4 structures insights into business frameworks.

📌 **Cybersecurity**

🎯 *Threat assessment briefing*

🧠 **Prompt:** *"Simulate a cybersecurity threat scenario targeting a fintech company. Outline likely attack vectors, impact analysis, and recommended mitigation steps."*

👹 **Best For: Claude, GPT-4**

✅ **Why:**

- Claude handles scenario planning.
- GPT-4 synthesizes real-world security knowledge into briefings.

4.5   Fine-Tuning Prompts for More Accurate AI Responses

When AI responses **aren't accurate**, use these **prompt tuning techniques**:

1. Add More Context

❌ **Bad Prompt:** *"Tell me about climate change."*

✅ **Better Prompt:** *"Explain the impact of climate change on agriculture, with a focus on drought conditions and shifting crop yields."*

2. Request a Step-by-Step Answer

✕ **Bad Prompt:** *"How does quantum computing work?"*

☑ **Better Prompt:** *"Explain quantum computing as if you are teaching a high school student. Use step-by-step explanations and simple analogies."*

3. Specify the Output Format

✕ **Bad Prompt:** *"List AI companies."*

☑ **Better Prompt:** *"Provide a table of the top five AI companies, including their founding year, CEO, and major AI innovation."*

📌 **Expected Output:**

Company	Founding Year	CEO	Key Innovation
OpenAI	2015	Sam Altman	GPT-4, DALL·E
DeepMind	2010	Demis Hassabis	AlphaFold, AlphaGo

4.6   Hands-On Exercises: Test Your Prompt Optimization Skills!

✏ **Exercise 1:**

- Rewrite this **generic** prompt for **GPT-4 optimization**:
- ✕ *"Write about space exploration."*
- ☑ **Your Improved Prompt:** _______________

✏ **Exercise 2:**

- Create a **role-based prompt for Claude** about AI and ethics.

✏ **Exercise 3:**

- Optimize this prompt for **Gemini's strength in factual accuracy**:
- ✕ *"What are the top emerging AI startups?"*
- ☑ **Your Improved Prompt:** _______________

4.7   Summary & Key Takeaways

✔ Different AI models have **unique strengths and limitations**.

✔ **Optimizing prompts** ensure **better accuracy, depth, and efficiency**.

✔ Use **structured, role-based, and CoT prompts** for maximum effectiveness.

✔ **Fine-tune** prompts by **adding context, specifying formats, and breaking down complex queries**.

✔ Experiment with **industry-specific AI prompt techniques** to get superior results.

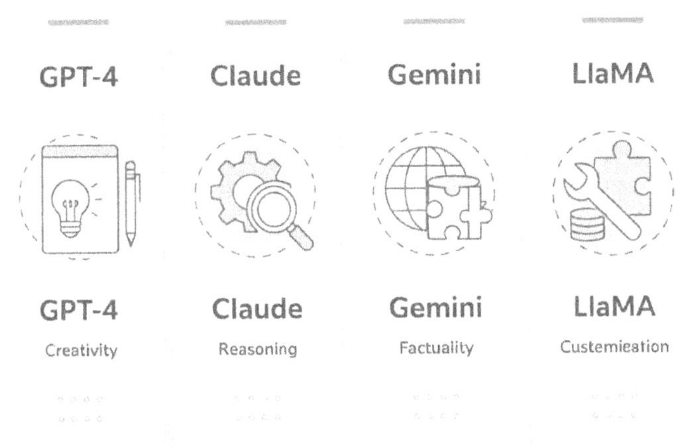

Figure 4.1: Model to be used based on task

🚀 What's Next?

Now that you understand **how to optimize prompts for different AI models**, the next chapter will cover **AI in Creative Applications**, including:

✔ **AI in Content Writing & Storytelling**.

✔ **Using Prompts for AI Art & Video Generation**.

✔ **Creative Applications in Music & Design**.

You know, why the below solution is provided?

🖉 **Solution 1:**

☑ **Your Improved Prompt (GPT-4):**

"Write a detailed blog post on the history and future of space exploration, covering key milestones like the Moon landing, the rise of private space companies (e.g., SpaceX), and upcoming missions to Mars. Use a conversational tone aimed at curious high school students."

☑ **Why It Works:**

- Gives structure (history, present, future).
- Defines audience and tone.
- Leverages GPT-4's strength in engaging storytelling with factual coherence.

🖉 **Solution 2: Role-Based Prompt for Claude – AI & Ethics**

☑ **Your Improved Prompt (Claude):**

"You are an AI ethics professor preparing a lecture for graduate students. Explain the ethical implications of using facial recognition technology in public surveillance. Include both arguments for its use and concerns about privacy, bias, and regulation."

☑ **Why It Works:**

- Assigns a **clear role** (ethics professor).
- Specifies **context** (lecture, graduate students).
- Promotes **balanced reasoning**, aligned with Claude's strength in thoughtful, nuanced responses.

🖊 Solution 3: Gemini – Optimize for Factual Accuracy

☑ Your Improved Prompt (Gemini):

"List the top emerging AI startups as of Q2 2025, including their primary innovations, funding rounds, and notable partnerships. Focus on factual data from credible sources."

☑ Why It Works:

- Adds **time sensitivity** (Q2 2025).
- Requests **specific data points** (funding, partnerships).
- Emphasizes **credibility**, playing to Gemini's strength in up-to-date, fact-based analysis.

CHAPTER 5

Creative Applications of Prompt Engineering

5.1 Introduction

AI is no longer limited to automation and data analysis—it is now a **creative powerhouse** capable of generating **stories, art, music, videos, and even interactive experiences**. Through prompt engineering, users can harness AI models to **enhance creativity, streamline workflows, and bring imaginative ideas to life**.

This chapter explores **how AI-powered creativity works**, the best **prompting techniques for storytelling, art, and music**, and real-world examples of **AI-driven content creation**.

5.2 How AI Powers Creativity

AI models like **GPT-4, DALL·E, MidJourney, and Suno AI** use **pattern recognition, deep learning, and generative models** to create unique content based on structured prompts.

Creative Domain	Best AI Model	Common Use Cases
Storytelling & Writing	GPT-4, Claude	Fiction, scripts, poetry, essays
AI Art & Design	DALL·E, MidJourney	Digital artwork, concept art, design mockups
Music Generation	Suno AI, AIVA, OpenAI Jukebox	AI-composed music, soundtracks, beats
Video Production	Runway ML, Pika Labs	AI-generated video effects, animations

5.3   Storytelling & Content Writing with AI

AI-powered storytelling has evolved from simple text generation to **dynamic narratives, poetry, and scriptwriting**.

1. Role-Based Storytelling Prompts

📌 **Example:**

📝 **Prompt:**

"You are a science fiction writer. Write a short story (300 words) about a lost astronaut discovering an alien civilization on a distant planet. Include suspense and dialogue."

✅ **Why It Works:**

- Assigns **AI a role** (sci-fi writer).
- Specifies **word count and storytelling elements**.

2. Character & Plot Development Prompts

📌 **Example:**

📝 **Prompt:**

"Create a detailed character profile for a cyberpunk hacker living in a futuristic megacity. Include name, background, skills, weaknesses, and motivations."

📌 **Expected Output:**

Attribute	Details
Name	Nova Ryker
Background	Orphan raised by underground hackers
Skills	Cybersecurity, AI programming, social engineering
Weaknesses	Distrustful, impulsive
Motivations	Exposing corporate corruption

☑ **Why It Works:**

- Defines **specific elements** for character creation.
- Provides **structured output**.

3. Poetry & Songwriting with AI

📌 **Example:**

📝 **Prompt:**

"Write a romantic poem in the style of Shakespeare about love lost and found again."

📌 **Example Output (Excerpt):**

"Upon the shores where memories sleep,

I wandered, longing, lost and deep..."

☑ **Why It Works:**

- Defines **tone and poetic style**.
- AI adjusts its language to match **Shakespearean English**.

5.4   AI Art & Image Generation

AI art platforms like **DALL·E and MidJourney** generate unique visuals from text prompts. The key to **stunning AI artwork** is **descriptive, structured prompts**.

1. Structuring AI Art Prompts

📌 **Example:**

📝 **Prompt:**

"A cyberpunk cityscape at night, neon lights reflecting off the rain-soaked streets, a hooded figure standing under a flickering street lamp. Style: Futuristic realism."

✅ **Why It Works:**

- Defines **setting (cyberpunk city at night).**
- Specifies **atmosphere (neon lights, rain-soaked streets).**
- Includes **art style (futuristic realism).**

📌 **Example Output:**

[AI-generated cyberpunk cityscape]

2. AI-Generated Concept Art for Movies & Games

📌 **Example:**

📝 **Prompt:**

"A medieval warrior in battle, clad in silver armor, wielding a flaming sword, set against a stormy sky. Style: Dark fantasy illustration."

📌 **Expected Output:**

- A **highly detailed** fantasy warrior.
- **Dramatic lighting and color contrast.**

✅ **Why It Works:**

- Uses **visual and stylistic descriptors.**
- Matches **a specific art genre (dark fantasy).**

5.5　AI Music & Soundtrack Generation

AI-generated music is becoming **increasingly sophisticated**, used in **movies, video games, and marketing.**

1. Creating AI Music with Suno AI & AIVA

📌 **Example:**

📝 **Prompt:**

"Generate a cinematic orchestral soundtrack with a rising crescendo, similar to Hans Zimmer's style, for a space exploration documentary."

☑️ **Why It Works:**

- Defines **music genre (orchestral).**
- Requests **specific stylistic inspiration (Hans Zimmer).**

📌 **Example Output:**

- 🎵 A dramatic orchestral score, building tension.

5.6   AI Video Generation & Animation

AI video tools like **Runway ML and Pika Labs** generate **animated scenes, VFX, and AI-driven cinematography.**

1. AI-Powered Video Scene Generation

📌 **Example:**

📝 **Prompt:**

"Generate a cinematic video sequence of a futuristic city with flying cars, atmospheric lighting, and a sweeping camera motion."

📌 **Expected Output:**

- A **high-quality 3D-rendered animation.**
- **Realistic motion effects.**

☑️ **Why It Works:**

- Defines **scene details (futuristic city, flying cars).**
- Requests **a specific cinematic motion style.**

5.7   Real-World Applications of AI Creativity

📌 **Marketing & Advertising**

- AI-generated **ad copy, social media posts, commercial scripts.**
- Example: **AI-written Coca-Cola ad campaigns.**

📌 Gaming & Film Production

- AI-generated **game concept art, character design, VFX**.
- Example: **AI-enhanced backgrounds in Hollywood films**.

📌 Music Industry

- AI-assisted **beat-making, personalized music composition**.
- Example: **AI-generated album cover art & lyrics**.

5.8   Hands-On Exercises: Try These Creative Prompts!

✏️ Exercise 1:

- Generate a **short horror story prompt** for GPT-4.
- ✖ *"Write a scary story."*
- ✅ **Your Improved Prompt:** ________________

✏️ Exercise 2:

- Write an **AI art prompt** for a **fantasy illustration**.
- ✖ *"Draw a dragon."*
- ✅ **Your Improved Prompt:** ________________

✏️ Exercise 3:

- Create an **AI music generation prompt** for a **jazz composition**.
- ✖ *"Make a jazz song."*
- ✅ **Your Improved Prompt:** ________________

5.9   Summary & Key Takeaways

✔ **AI creativity is transforming content creation in writing, music, art, and video.**

✔ **Role-based storytelling and structured character prompts enhance AI-generated narratives.**

✔ **Descriptive AI art prompts produce high-quality digital artwork.**

✔ **Music generation prompts need specific instruments, tempo, and stylistic references.**

✔ **AI video tools enable automated cinematography and visual effects.**

Figure 5.1: Creative applications of prompt engineering

🚀 What's Next?

Now that you've explored **AI's creative applications**, the next chapter will focus on **AI in Business & Automation**, covering:

✔ **Automating workflows with AI-powered prompts.**

✔ **AI-driven customer support, chatbots, and sales automation.**

✔ **Case studies on AI in marketing, HR, and finance.**

CHAPTER 6

AI in Business – Automating Workflows

6.1   Introduction

AI-powered automation is transforming businesses by **reducing manual effort, improving efficiency, and enabling faster decision-making**. Organizations now use **prompt-driven AI** to automate:

- ✔ **Customer Support** (AI chatbots, virtual assistants)

- ✔ **Sales & Marketing** (AI-generated content, email automation)

- ✔ **HR & Recruitment** (Resume screening, interview scheduling)

- ✔ **Finance & Data Analysis** (AI-driven financial insights, fraud detection)

This chapter explores **how prompt engineering optimizes AI automation in business**, with real-world applications and practical examples.

6.2   How AI-Powered Automation Works

AI-driven business automation works by combining:

Natural Language Processing (NLP) – AI understands human input and generates meaningful responses.

Machine Learning (ML) – AI learns from past interactions to improve accuracy.

Process Automation – AI integrates with workflows to handle repetitive tasks.

📌 **Example:** AI in **Customer Support**

- Before: Human agents manually handle thousands of queries.
- After: AI **chatbots** respond instantly, resolving **80% of routine questions**.

6.3   Automating Customer Support with AI Chatbots

AI chatbots powered by **prompt engineering** handle:

✔ Customer inquiries **(FAQs, troubleshooting, billing issues)**

✔ Product recommendations **(personalized suggestions)**

✔ Complaint resolution **(AI detects sentiment, escalates urgent issues)**

Structuring AI Chatbot Prompts for Better Responses

📌 **Example: AI Customer Service Chatbot**

📝 **Prompt:**

"You are an AI customer support agent for an e-commerce store. A customer asks about a delayed order. Provide a professional and empathetic response."

📌 **Expected AI Response:**

"I sincerely apologize for the delay in your order. Due to high demand, shipments are taking longer than usual. I've checked your order status, and it will arrive within 3 days. Let me know if you need further assistance!"

☑ **Why It Works:**

✔ **Empathy & professionalism** included.

✔ **Specific information** provided.

6.4   AI in Marketing & Sales Automation

AI helps businesses **generate leads, create marketing content, and personalize outreach**.

📌 **Example: AI-Generated Marketing Email**

📝 **Prompt:**

"Write a persuasive marketing email for a 20% discount on our premium software plan. Keep it engaging and action-driven."

📌 **AI Response (Email Example):**

Subject: Unlock 20% Off – Limited Time Offer!

🚀 **Upgrade Your Experience with 20% Off!**

Dear [Customer],

We're offering an exclusive **20% discount** on our premium plan for a limited time. Get advanced features and **boost productivity effortlessly**.

Claim your discount now before it's gone!

[Upgrade Now]

Best,

The [Company] Team

☑ **Why It Works:**

✔ **Persuasive & engaging tone**

✔ **Call-to-action (Upgrade Now)**

6.5   AI-Powered HR & Recruitment Automation

HR teams use AI for **resume screening, interview scheduling, and employee onboarding**.

📌 **Example: AI Resume Screening Prompt**

📝 **Prompt:**

"You are an AI hiring assistant. Analyze the following resume and rank the candidate's suitability for a data analyst position based on required skills."

📌 **Expected Output:**

Candidate Name	Skill Match (%)	Strengths	Concerns
John Doe	85%	Strong Python, SQL skills	Limited project experience
Jane Smith	92%	Advanced data visualization, ML expertise	None

✅ **Why It Works:**

✔ **AI ranks candidates based on skills.**

✔ **HR can make informed hiring decisions faster.**

6.6   AI in Finance & Data Analytics

AI-driven financial automation helps with:

✔ **Fraud Detection** (AI detects unusual transactions)

✔ **Financial Forecasting** (AI predicts revenue trends)

✔ **Expense Management** (Automates invoice approvals)

📌 **Example: AI Financial Report Generation**

📝 **Prompt:**

"Generate a financial report summarizing Q2 revenue trends, key growth areas, and potential risks. Use a structured format."

📌 **Expected Output:**

Q2 Financial Summary

📈 **Revenue Growth:** 12% increase

📊 **Top Growth Sectors:** SaaS, Retail

⚠️ **Risks Identified:** Higher operational costs

✅ **Why It Works:**

✔ **Structured financial insights**

✔ **AI detects trends and risk areas**

6.7   Case Studies: Real-World AI Business Automation

📌 **Case Study 1: AI in Customer Support – Amazon's AI Chatbot**

✅ **Impact:** Reduced human workload by **60%** while improving response time.

📌 **Case Study 2: AI in Finance – PayPal's Fraud Detection**

✅ **Impact:** AI detects **fraudulent transactions 95% faster** than traditional systems.

📌 **Case Study 3: AI in Marketing – Netflix's AI Personalization**

✅ **Impact:** AI-driven recommendations **increase watch time by 70%.**

6.8   Hands-On Exercises: AI Business Prompting

✏️ **Exercise 1:**

- Rewrite this **basic chatbot prompt** into a **more structured** prompt:
- ✖ *"Help a customer with login issues."*
- ✅ **Your Improved Prompt:** ______________

✎ Exercise 2:

- Create a **role-based AI marketing prompt** for a **new product launch**.

✎ Exercise 3:

- Write a **structured AI financial analysis prompt** for an annual business report.

6.9   Summary & Key Takeaways

✔ **AI automation improves efficiency in customer support, HR, marketing, and finance.**

✔ **Structured prompts generate better business insights.**

✔ **AI-powered chatbots handle routine queries, reducing workload.**

✔ **Real-world companies like Amazon, Netflix, and PayPal use AI-driven automation.**

✔ **Well-crafted AI prompts lead to accurate and professional business communication.**

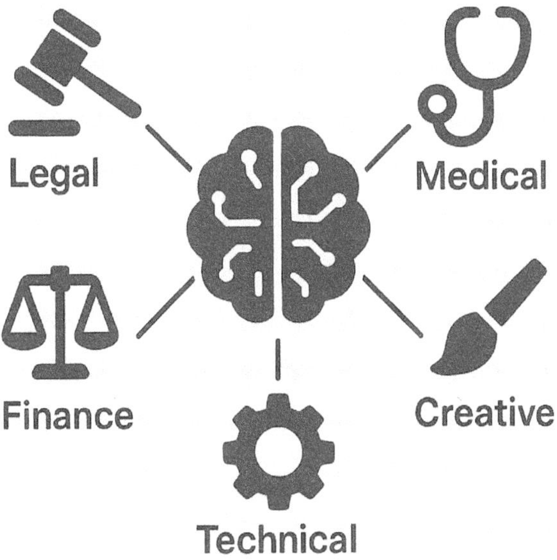

Figure 6.1: Domain specific prompt engineering

AI in Business – Automating Workflows

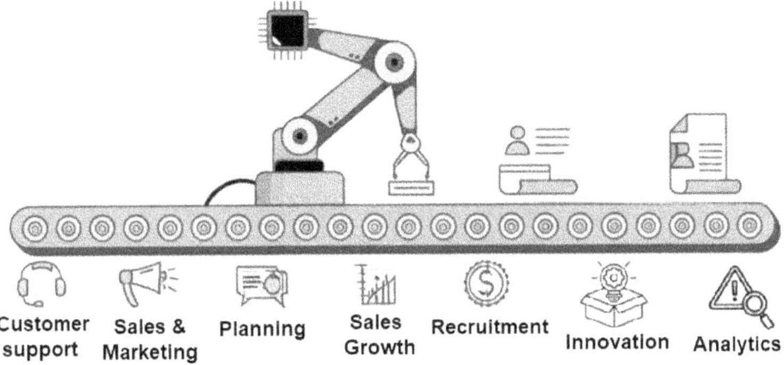

Figure 6.2 Automating workflows using AI

🚀 What's Next?

Now that you've explored **AI-powered business automation**, the next chapter will focus on **AI Ethics & Bias**, covering:

✔ **Avoiding biased AI-generated responses.**

✔ **Ensuring ethical AI decision-making in business & law.**

✔ **Real-world ethical dilemmas in AI automation.**

Solution to the Exercise:

✏️ Exercise 1

✅ Your Improved Prompt:

"You are a customer support chatbot for a banking app. Assist a user who is unable to log into their account. First, confirm their identity with security questions, then guide them through password recovery. If unresolved, escalate the issue to a human agent."

💡 Why It Works:

✅ Defines role and system (banking app chatbot)

✅ Structures flow (verify → assist → escalate)

✅ Sets boundaries (security and escalation)

✏️ Exercise 2: Role-Based AI Marketing Prompt (Product Launch)

✅ Your Improved Prompt:

"You are a senior brand strategist launching a new plant-based protein drink targeted at Gen Z. Create a 3-part social media campaign including a hook (short video idea), an influencer strategy, and a CTA that encourages user-generated content. Keep it witty, eco-conscious, and on-trend with Gen Z values."

💡 **Why It Works:**

✅ Assigns a role (brand strategist)

✅ Defines product, audience & tone

✅ Structures content by deliverables (video, influencers, CTA)

✏️ **Exercise 3: Structured AI Financial Analysis Prompt (Annual Report)**

✅ Your Improved Prompt:

"Analyze the 2024 annual report of a mid-sized SaaS company. Provide a summary of key financial metrics (revenue, net profit, YoY growth), identify areas of concern, and suggest strategic recommendations for improving profitability in 2025."

💡 Why It Works:

✅ Sets data context (2024 report)

✅ Defines metrics to extract

✅ Encourages forward-looking insights (strategic action)

CHAPTER 7

AI Ethics & Bias in Prompt Engineering

7.1   Introduction

As AI becomes more integrated into daily life and business, concerns about **ethics, fairness, and bias** have emerged. AI models are trained on vast datasets, but if these datasets contain **biased, misleading, or incomplete** information, the AI can **reinforce stereotypes, make unfair decisions, or spread misinformation.**

Key Ethical Concerns in AI Prompt Engineering

✔ **Bias in AI Responses** – AI may favor certain viewpoints based on its training data.

✔ **Misinformation & Hallucinations** – AI can generate false but convincing information.

✔ **Privacy & Data Security** – AI must handle user data responsibly.

✔ **Transparency & Accountability** – AI decisions should be explainable and fair.

This chapter explores **how AI bias happens**, how to **craft unbiased prompts**, and how to ensure **ethical AI usage** in business, education, and public decision-making.

7.2   Understanding AI Bias and Its Causes

AI bias occurs when an AI model produces **unfair, misleading, or discriminatory outputs** due to biases in its training data.

📌 Example of AI Bias in Hiring

- An AI **resume screening system** trained on historical hiring data **rejects female applicants** because past hiring patterns favored men.

📌 Example of AI Bias in Facial Recognition

- Some AI facial recognition models have **higher error rates** when identifying people of color due to **underrepresentation in training data**.

How Bias Creeps into AI Models

Bias Source	How It Affects AI	Example
Historical Data Bias	AI learns from biased past decisions	Biased hiring patterns
Selection Bias	AI is trained on non-representative datasets	Poor accuracy for minority groups
Algorithmic Bias	Model prioritizes certain responses	AI over-favors one political view
User Interaction Bias	AI adapts to user preferences	AI amplifies extreme opinions

📌 **Key Takeaway:** AI is only as fair as the data it's trained on. Prompt engineers must **counteract bias** through careful prompt design.

7.3 How to Detect and Reduce AI Bias in Prompts

1. Avoiding Loaded or Leading Prompts

❌ **Bad Prompt:** *"Why are electric cars better than gas cars?"*

✅ **Improved Prompt:** *"Compare the advantages and disadvantages of electric and gas-powered cars."*

📌 **Why It Works:**

✔ Removes **bias toward electric cars**.

✔ Encourages a **balanced response**.

2. Requesting Multiple Perspectives

✘ **Bad Prompt:** *"What are the problems with renewable energy?"*

☑ **Improved Prompt:** *"Discuss both the benefits and challenges of renewable energy in modern economies."*

📌 **Why It Works:**

✔ Encourages a **neutral and fact-based answer**.

✔ AI is less likely to generate **one-sided arguments**.

3. Fact-Checking AI Responses for Misinformation

📌 **Example:**

📝 **Prompt:** *"Summarize the causes of climate change."*

📌 **Possible AI Issue:**

- AI **hallucinates false information** (e.g., "volcanic eruptions are the primary cause of climate change").

☑ **How to Fix It:**

- Ask AI to **cite sources**:
- 📝 **Revised Prompt:** *"Summarize the causes of climate change with references to scientific studies."*

📌 **Why It Works:**

✔ AI is **forced to rely on verifiable data**.

✔ Reduces the chances of **false information**.

7.4   Ethical AI in Business & Decision-Making

Businesses using AI for hiring, lending, and legal decisions must ensure **fair and unbiased outcomes**.

📌 **Example: Ethical AI in Hiring**

📝 **Prompt:**

"You are an AI hiring assistant. Analyze job applications based on skills and experience only. Do not consider race, gender, or age."

✅ **Why It Works:**

✔ Eliminates **demographic biases**.

✔ Ensures **skill-based hiring**.

7.5   AI & Privacy: Handling Sensitive Data Responsibly

AI systems must protect user privacy by **not storing or misusing sensitive data**.

📌 **Example of Unethical AI Use:**

- **Chatbots storing personal medical data** without user consent.

✅ **How to Ensure AI Privacy Compliance**

- Avoid collecting unnecessary user data.
- Use GDPR-compliant AI models.
- Provide transparency in AI decisions.

📌 **Example: Ethical AI Prompt for Data Privacy**

📝 **Prompt:**

"You are an AI customer support agent. Answer user queries without collecting or storing personal data."

☑ **Why It Works:**

✔ Ensures **data protection**.

✔ Prevents **privacy violations**.

7.6   Case Studies: AI Ethics in the Real World

📌 **Case Study 1: AI Hiring Bias – Amazon's Resume Screening AI**

⬤ **Problem:** AI favored male applicants over female applicants due to biased training data.

☑ **Solution:** Amazon had to **redesign the AI** to remove gender-based bias.

📌 **Case Study 2: AI Misinformation – Google's AI Chatbot Hallucinations**

⬤ **Problem:** AI-generated **fake news articles** due to biased data sources.

☑ **Solution:** Google **improved AI fact-checking** to minimize false claims.

📌 **Case Study 3: Ethical AI in Finance – AI Loan Approval Systems**

⬤ **Problem:** AI rejected **minority applicants** for loans due to biased historical data.

☑ **Solution:** Lenders used **fairness-aware algorithms** to correct discrimination.

7.7   Hands-On Exercises: AI Ethics & Bias in Prompting

✏ **Exercise 1:**

- Rewrite this **biased prompt** to make it more neutral:
- ✗ *"Why is remote work better than office work?"*
- ☑ **Your Improved Prompt:** _______________

✏️ Exercise 2:

- Create a **fact-checking AI prompt** for verifying health information.

✏️ Exercise 3:

- Design an **AI hiring prompt** that avoids demographic bias.

7.8   Summary & Key Takeaways

✔️ AI bias is a serious issue that affects hiring, finance, law, and social media.

✔️ Ethical AI requires careful prompt engineering to avoid biased, misleading, or discriminatory outputs.

✔️ Fact-checking AI responses is essential to prevent misinformation.

✔️ Privacy-conscious AI prompts help ensure data protection.

✔️ Real-world AI bias cases highlight the importance of fair and responsible AI use.

Figure 7.1: AI Ethics & Bias in prompt engineering

🚀 What's Next?

Now that you understand **AI ethics and bias**, the next chapter will explore **how to evaluate and improve AI prompt performance**, covering:

- ✔ How to test AI-generated responses for quality.

- ✔ Measuring accuracy, creativity, and reliability.

- ✔ Optimizing prompts for better outputs.

Solution to the exercise

✏️ Exercise 1:

☑ Your Improved Prompt:

"Compare the advantages and challenges of remote work and office work from the perspective of employee productivity, collaboration, and well-being."

💡 Why It Works:

- ☑ Neutral framing

- ☑ Encourages balanced evaluation

- ☑ Avoids leading language or assumed preference

✏️ Exercise 2: Fact-Checking Health Prompt

☑ Your Improved Prompt:

"Verify the accuracy of the following health claim: 'Drinking green tea daily reduces the risk of heart disease.' Provide evidence from credible medical sources such as WHO, CDC, or peer-reviewed journals."

💡 Why It Works:

- ☑ Anchors fact-checking to **credible sources**

✅ Focuses on a **specific health claim**

✅ Promotes **evidence-based reasoning**

✏️ **Exercise 3: Bias-Aware Hiring Prompt**

✅ **Your Improved Prompt:**

"Evaluate these anonymized candidate profiles for a software engineering role based on relevant skills, project experience, and problem-solving abilities. Do not consider demographic details or personal identifiers in your analysis."

💡 **Why It Works:**

✅ Prioritizes **skill-based evaluation**

✅ Explicitly **removes demographic bias**

✅ Reinforces ethical prompting in HR use cases

CHAPTER 8

Measuring and Improving Prompt Performance

8.1   Introduction

AI-generated responses vary in **accuracy, relevance, clarity, and creativity**. Some prompts produce **precise and structured** outputs, while others lead to **inconsistent, biased, or irrelevant** responses.

To ensure **high-quality AI outputs**, prompt engineers need to:

✔ Evaluate response quality using key performance metrics.

✔ Refine prompts for better clarity, accuracy, and efficiency.

✔ Optimize AI-generated responses based on feedback and testing.

This chapter covers **how to measure prompt performance**, **common challenges**, and **techniques to improve AI-generated outputs** for various applications.

8.2   Key Metrics for Evaluating AI Responses

To determine **whether an AI-generated response is effective**, evaluate it based on the following metrics:

Metric	Description	Example
Accuracy	Is the information correct and fact-based?	Does the AI provide the right definition of a concept?
Relevance	Does the response match the user's intent?	Does AI answer the specific question asked?
Clarity	Is the response easy to understand?	Is the explanation well-structured and free of jargon?
Creativity	Does AI provide unique and insightful content?	Is AI generating original ideas rather than repeating common ones?
Conciseness	Is the response clear without unnecessary details?	Does AI avoid redundant or overly long explanations?

📌 **Example:** Evaluating AI's Response to a Prompt

📝 **Prompt:** *"Explain blockchain in simple terms for a beginner."*

📌 **AI Response Evaluation:**

✔ **Accuracy:** ☑ Correct definition given.

✔ **Relevance:** ☑ AI focuses on blockchain basics.

✔ **Clarity:** ⚠ Uses some complex jargon.

✔ **Creativity:** ☑ Engaging real-world example used.

✔ **Conciseness:** ⚠ Could be more concise.

☑ **Final Score: 8/10** (Needs improvement in clarity and conciseness.)

8.3   Common Problems in AI-Generated Responses

Even with structured prompts, AI can generate **suboptimal responses**. Here are some common issues:

1. Overly Generic or Vague Responses

✗ Bad AI Response:

"Technology is changing the world in many ways."

☑ Improved Prompt:

"Provide three specific ways AI is transforming the healthcare industry, with real-world examples."

📌 Why It Works:

✔ Forces AI to be **specific**.

✔ Ensures AI gives **real-world examples**.

2. Factually Incorrect or Misleading Responses

✗ Bad AI Response:

"The Eiffel Tower was built in 1950." (Incorrect)

☑ Improved Prompt:

"When was the Eiffel Tower built? Cite sources where possible."

📌 Why It Works:

✔ AI will **fact-check** before responding.

✔ **Reduces misinformation** risk.

3. Overly Long or Redundant Responses

✗ Bad AI Response:

"Artificial Intelligence is a field of study that involves machines performing tasks that typically require human intelligence, such as language processing, problem-solving, and decision-making. AI includes machine learning, which is a subset of AI that allows computers to learn from data without being explicitly programmed. AI also includes deep

learning, which is a type of machine learning that uses neural networks to process complex data."

✅ **Improved Prompt:**

"Explain AI in two sentences for a general audience."

📌 **Why It Works:**

✔ **Forces AI to be concise**.

✔ Keeps the answer **accessible to all audiences**.

8.4   Techniques to Improve Prompt Performance

1. Use Step-by-Step Instructions

📝 **Prompt:**

"Explain how Bitcoin transactions work in five clear steps."

📌 **Expected AI Response:**

1. User sends Bitcoin to another wallet.
2. The transaction is broadcasted to the Bitcoin network.
3. Miners verify the transaction using cryptographic algorithms.
4. Verified transactions are added to the blockchain ledger.
5. The receiver gets the Bitcoin after network confirmation.

✅ **Why It Works:**

✔ Breaks complex topics into easy steps.

✔ Improves clarity and structure.

2. Ask for Multiple Answers or Perspectives

📝 Prompt:

"List three benefits and three risks of using AI in finance."

📌 Expected AI Response:

✔ Benefits:

1. Faster decision-making.
2. Improved fraud detection.
3. Reduced human error.

✔ Risks:

1. Algorithmic bias.
2. Data privacy concerns.
3. High dependence on technology.

☑ Why It Works:

✔ Ensures a **balanced AI response**.

✔ Encourages **critical thinking** in AI outputs.

3. Use Contextual or Role-Based Prompts

📝 Prompt:

"You are a career coach. Provide three tips for a college graduate entering the AI industry."

📌 Expected AI Response:

1. Build strong Python and machine learning skills.
2. Work on AI projects and contribute to open-source platforms.
3. Stay updated with AI research by following industry experts.

✅ **Why It Works:**

✔️ AI **tailors the response** to the target audience.

✔️ AI **mimics expert advice** effectively.

8.5   Testing and Iterating for Better AI Prompts

To optimize a prompt, **test different versions** and **analyze the AI's responses**.

Example: Iterating on a Prompt

✗ **First Attempt:**

"Tell me about space travel." (Too broad)

✅ **Second Attempt:**

"Explain three challenges of space travel and how astronauts overcome them." (More structured)

✅ **Third Attempt:**

"Explain three challenges of space travel (zero gravity, radiation, and isolation) and provide NASA's solutions for each." (Best version)

📌 **Key Takeaway:** Refining prompts **step-by-step** improves **response quality and depth**.

8.6   Case Studies: Improving AI Performance with Prompt Engineering

📌 **Case Study 1: AI Chatbot Optimization (Customer Service)**

🔘 **Problem:** AI chatbot responses were too generic.

✅ **Solution:** The company used **step-by-step prompts and role-based AI guidance** to **improve customer satisfaction by 40%**.

📌 **Case Study 2: AI for Legal Analysis**

⬤ **Problem:** AI generated **biased legal opinions** based on limited training data.

☑ **Solution:** Lawyers **fine-tuned prompts** to require AI to **list arguments from multiple legal perspectives**.

📌 **Case Study 3: AI in Education**

⬤ **Problem:** AI explanations were **too advanced** for students.

☑ **Solution:** Teachers **rewrote prompts** to specify **grade level and required explanation simplicity**.

8.7   Hands-On Exercises: Test Your Prompt Optimization Skills!

✏ **Exercise 1:**

- Rewrite this **vague prompt** to make it more structured:
- ✖ *"Tell me about machine learning."*
- ☑ **Your Improved Prompt:** _______________

✏ **Exercise 2:**

- Modify this **long-winded AI response** into a **concise answer**.

✏ **Exercise 3:**

- Create a **step-by-step AI prompt** for explaining **how self-driving cars work**.

8.8   Summary & Key Takeaways

✔ AI-generated responses should be evaluated based on accuracy, relevance, clarity, creativity, and conciseness.

✔ Common AI response issues include vagueness, factual errors, and redundancy.

✔ Step-by-step instructions, role-based prompts, and multiple-perspective prompts improve AI output.

✔ Testing and iterating on prompts leads to better AI-generated responses.

✔ Case studies show real-world success in improving AI performance using prompt engineering.

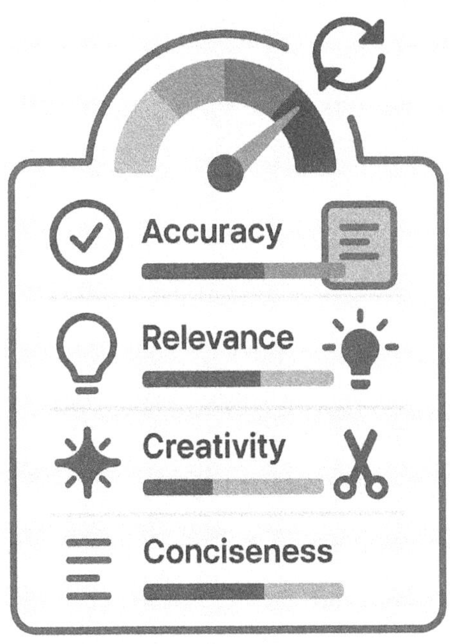

Figure 8.1: Measuring and improving prompt performance

🚀 What's Next?

Now that you've mastered **evaluating and improving prompt performance**, the next chapter will focus on **The Future of Prompt Engineering**, covering:

- ✔ Emerging AI prompting trends.

- ✔ AutoGPT and AI-driven self-prompting.

- ✔ How AI models are evolving in understanding prompts.

Solution to Exercise

🖊 Exercise 1: Structure the Vague Prompt

✅ Your Improved Prompt:

"Explain the concept of machine learning to a non-technical audience. Include the types of machine learning (supervised, unsupervised, reinforcement), real-world examples, and why it's important in today's technology landscape."

💡 Why It Works:

- ✅ Clear audience definition (non-technical)

- ✅ Structured content (types, examples, significance)

- ✅ Supports informative + approachable output

🖊 Exercise 2: Make AI Response Concise

✖ Original Long-Winded Response (example):

"Self-driving cars use a variety of technologies such as LiDAR, cameras, and radar sensors along with advanced AI models and machine learning algorithms that are trained on massive datasets collected from millions of driving miles in different conditions. These models are able to interpret the road environment, make decisions, and perform driving maneuvers, sometimes better than humans."

☑ Improved Concise Version:

"Self-driving cars use sensors and AI to detect surroundings, make decisions, and navigate roads—mimicking human driving with data-trained precision."

💡 Why It Works:

☑ Short, punchy, and retains meaning

☑ Great for summaries, headlines, or executive briefings

✎ Exercise 3: Step-by-Step Prompt — Self-Driving Cars

☑ Your Improved Prompt:

"Explain how self-driving cars work in a step-by-step manner. Break it down into stages: (1) sensing the environment, (2) interpreting data, (3) making decisions, and (4) executing actions. Use simple language and include a real-world example for each stage."

💡 Why It Works:

☑ Guides the AI through structured stages

☑ Improves clarity for learners

☑ Encourages example-based learning

CHAPTER 9

The Future of Prompt Engineering

9.1   Introduction

AI is rapidly evolving, and so is **prompt engineering**. As AI models become more **sophisticated, autonomous, and multimodal**, the way we **interact with AI** will shift from manual prompt crafting to **AI-driven self-prompting systems**.

Key Trends in the Future of Prompt Engineering

- ✔ AI will become better at understanding context and intent.

- ✔ AutoGPT and self-prompting AI will reduce human intervention.

- ✔ Multimodal AI will integrate text, images, and videos into a single prompt.

- ✔ Fine-tuned personal AI models will deliver customized experiences.

This chapter explores the **emerging trends in AI prompting** and how they will impact **business, automation, and creativity** in the coming years.

9.2   AI Models are Becoming More Context-Aware

Traditional AI Prompting (2020-2023)

- AI relies heavily on **clear and structured** prompts.
- Output quality depends on **user input precision**.

Next-Gen AI Prompting (2024 & Beyond)

- AI **understands user intent** even with vague prompts.
- AI **remembers previous conversations** (persistent memory).
- AI **auto-adjusts** its response style based on the user.

📌 Example of Context-Aware AI

📝 Old AI Model (GPT-3.5)

❌ **Prompt:** *"Explain relativity."*

🔻 **AI Response:** *"Relativity is a theory in physics proposed by Albert Einstein..."*

📝 New AI Model (GPT-5 or Future AI)

✅ **Prompt:** *"I'm an 8th-grade student. Explain relativity using a fun analogy."*

◈ **AI Response:** *"Imagine you're on a spaceship traveling at near-light speed. Time slows down for you compared to your friend on Earth..."*

✅ **Why It Works:**

✔ AI **adapts its response** based on the user's background.

✔ AI **remembers previous interactions** for personalization.

9.3   AutoGPT & Self-Prompting AI

What is AutoGPT?

- AutoGPT is an **AI agent that generates its own prompts** to complete tasks autonomously.
- Instead of a user giving a single prompt, AutoGPT **thinks, plans, and executes tasks** step by step.

📌 Example of AutoGPT in Action

📝 **Prompt:** *"Find the top 5 AI research papers on deep learning and summarize them."*

How AutoGPT Works:

1. AutoGPT **searches for the best papers**.
2. It **analyzes abstracts and key findings**.
3. It **creates a structured summary** with references.

✅ **Why It's Revolutionary:**

✔ **Minimizes human effort**—AI handles research tasks independently.

✔ **More accurate and structured outputs**.

📌 **Key Takeaway:** Future AI systems **won't just answer questions—they will solve complex problems autonomously**.

9.4   Multimodal AI: Combining Text, Images, and Video

AI is evolving from **text-only models** to **multimodal systems** that can process **text, images, audio, and video** in a single prompt.

📌 **Example of a Multimodal AI Prompt**

📝 **Prompt:**

"Analyze this image of a solar eclipse and explain the science behind it."

(Upload an image of an eclipse)

📌 **Expected AI Response:**

- AI **examines the image** to detect the eclipse.
- AI **explains the phenomenon** of light blocking.
- AI **generates a short educational video** on solar eclipses.

✅ **Why It's Powerful:**

✔ AI **understands visual context**, not just text.

✔ Enables **interactive and dynamic AI responses**.

📌 **Future Impact:** AI assistants will **process voice commands, analyze images, and generate video responses all within a single interaction**.

9.5   Personalized AI Models for Individuals & Businesses

AI models will soon become **customized to individual users** based on:

✔ Personal interests

✔ Preferred tone of response

✔ Learning style (text, audio, visual)

📌 **Example of Personalized AI Assistance**

📝 **User A:** *"Summarize this article for a tech audience."*

📝 **User B:** *"Summarize this article in simple terms for beginners."*

☑ **Future AI Response:**

- AI **adapts to the user's knowledge level**.
- AI **remembers past conversations** for personalization.

📌 **Key Takeaway:** Businesses will use **fine-tuned AI assistants** that match their **branding, customer needs, and internal workflows**.

9.6   Ethical Challenges in Future AI Prompting

As AI **gains more autonomy**, ethical concerns will become **more critical**.

Potential Risks of Advanced AI Prompting:

⚠ AI generating biased or misleading content.

⚠ Deepfake technology being misused.

⚠ Loss of transparency in AI decision-making.

📌 **How to Ensure Ethical AI Prompting:**

✔️ **Require AI to cite sources** when generating facts.

✔️ **Use transparency statements** in AI-generated content.

✔️ **Develop regulations for AI misuse prevention**.

📌 **Example of an Ethical AI Prompt**

📝 **Prompt:**

"Provide an unbiased comparison of electric vs. gasoline cars. Cite sources from neutral studies."

✅ **Why It Works:**

✔️ AI **avoids bias** in responses.

✔️ **Fact-checking** is built into the prompt.

📌 **Key Takeaway:** Ethical AI prompting **must balance creativity, accuracy, and responsibility**.

9.7   Case Studies: AI Prompting Innovations

📌 **Case Study 1: AutoGPT in Business Research**

⬤ **Problem:** Companies spend **weeks** manually researching competitors.

✅ **Solution:** AutoGPT scans market reports, extracts insights, and summarizes trends **in minutes**.

📌 **Case Study 2: Multimodal AI in Healthcare**

⬤ **Problem:** Doctors analyze **thousands of medical images** manually.

✅ **Solution:** AI scans images, detects diseases, and provides explanations **with 90% accuracy**.

📌 **Case Study 3: Personalized AI Assistants for Education**

⬤ **Problem:** Generic AI chatbots don't adapt to **individual learning styles**.

☑ **Solution:** AI tutors **adjust explanations based on student progress**.

📌 **Key Takeaway:** AI prompting is shifting from **static text-based outputs to dynamic, adaptive, and multimodal AI experiences**.

9.8   Hands-On Exercises: Future Prompt Engineering

✏ **Exercise 1:**

- Write a **self-prompting AI request** for an AI assistant handling **daily task management**.

✏ **Exercise 2:**

- Design a **multimodal AI prompt** that involves **text, images, and video generation**.

✏ **Exercise 3:**

- Create a **role-based AI prompt** for a **personalized AI learning assistant**.

9.9   Summary & Key Takeaways

✔ AI is becoming smarter, more autonomous, and multimodal.

✔ AutoGPT and self-prompting AI will handle tasks without manual input.

✔ Multimodal AI will integrate text, images, audio, and video for dynamic responses.

✔ Personalized AI assistants will tailor responses to users' needs.

✔ Ethical AI prompting will be crucial to prevent bias and misinformation.

📌 **Final Thought:** The future of prompt engineering isn't just about writing better prompts—it's about designing AI systems that think, adapt, and respond responsibly.

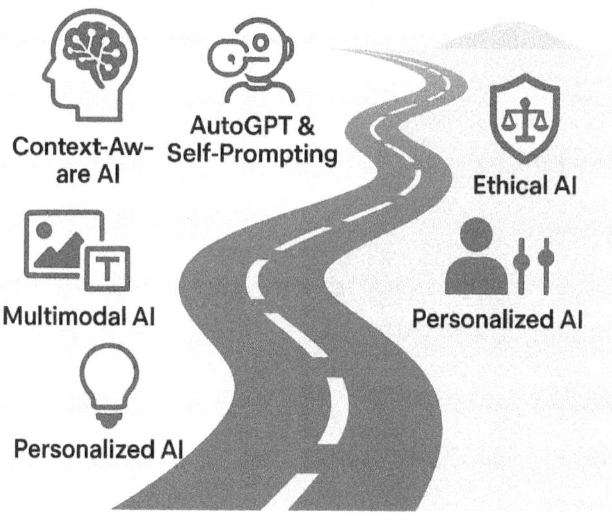

Figure 9.1: Future of Prompt Engineering

🚀 **What's Next?**

Now that we've explored the **future of prompt engineering**, the next chapter will provide **real-world case studies**, covering:

✔ How businesses and industries are applying AI prompting.

✔ Successful AI automation strategies.

✔ Lessons learned from real-world AI deployments.

Solution to the Exercise:

🖉 Exercise 1: Self-Prompting AI for Task Management

☑ Your Improved Prompt:

"You are an AI task assistant designed to plan and manage a user's day. Each morning, review the user's calendar, unread emails, and priority list. Then, generate a daily schedule, create reminders, and ask the user for missing inputs. Prompt yourself to re-check for updates hourly and reprioritize if needed."

💡 Why It Works:

☑ Introduces **self-directed logic loops**

☑ Allows AI to prompt itself for **adaptive updates**

☑ Mimics real assistant behavior with dynamic input handling

🖉 Exercise 2: Multimodal AI Prompt (Text + Image + Video)

☑ Your Improved Prompt:

*"Create a social media campaign for a new electric bike launch. Generate:

1. A 30-word punchy caption for Instagram
2. A product image of the bike in a modern city setting
3. A short video script (under 30 sec) highlighting eco-benefits and design features"*

💡 Why It Works:

☑ Engages multiple modalities (text + image + video)

☑ Suited for AI models with **image/video generation** (like Gemini or GPT-4 Turbo with vision)

☑ Real-world application (marketing) with structured deliverables

✏️ Exercise 3: Role-Based AI Learning Assistant

☑️ Your Improved Prompt:

"You are a personalized AI tutor for a college student studying computer science. Based on their recent quiz results and time availability, generate a weekly study plan focused on algorithms and data structures. Include daily learning goals, recommended resources, and quick review quizzes."

💡 Why It Works:

☑️ Role defined (AI tutor)

☑️ Personalization based on **performance + schedule**

☑️ Structured outcome (plan, goals, resources, quizzes)

CHAPTER 10

Case Studies of Successful Prompt Engineering

10.1   Introduction

AI-driven automation and **effective prompt engineering** are transforming industries worldwide. From **business and healthcare to finance and education**, organizations are leveraging AI prompts to:

- ✔ **Enhance efficiency** (reducing manual tasks)

- ✔ **Improve decision-making** (AI-driven insights)

- ✔ **Personalize customer experiences** (adaptive AI chatbots)

- ✔ **Automate content creation** (marketing, legal, research)

This chapter explores **real-world case studies** where **optimized prompts** have driven innovation, cost savings, and efficiency gains.

10.2   AI in Customer Support: Case Study – Amazon's AI Chatbots

📌 **Problem:**

Amazon faced **millions of customer queries daily**, leading to **long waiting times** for support.

📌 **Solution:**

Amazon deployed **AI chatbots** trained with **advanced prompts** to:

- Handle **frequent customer questions** (order tracking, refunds).
- Detect **customer sentiment** to escalate issues to human agents.
- Generate **personalized responses** based on order history.

📌 **Optimized AI Prompt Used:**

📝 **Prompt:**

"You are a customer support AI assistant for Amazon. A customer asks about a delayed order. Respond professionally, providing tracking details and an apology."

📌 **Results:**

✅ **70% of routine queries** were resolved by AI.

✅ **Customer response time was reduced** from **10 minutes to 30 seconds**.

📌 **Key Takeaway:**

✔ **Well-crafted prompts** enable AI chatbots to provide **fast, human-like responses**.

10.3 AI in Healthcare: Case Study – AI-Assisted Medical Diagnosis

📌 **Problem:**

Doctors at a leading hospital were **overwhelmed** with diagnosing thousands of X-rays, leading to **delays in patient treatment**.

📌 **Solution:**

The hospital used an **AI model** with **optimized diagnostic prompts** to:

- Analyze **X-ray images** and flag potential abnormalities.
- Suggest possible **diagnoses based on historical data**.
- Provide **explanations for medical professionals**.

📌 **Optimized AI Prompt Used:**

📝 **Prompt:**

"Analyze this X-ray for potential fractures. Provide a confidence score and explain why certain areas may indicate bone damage."

📌 **Results:**

✅ **Faster diagnosis** – AI-assisted screening reduced **review time by 60%**.

✅ **Improved accuracy** – AI correctly flagged **92% of fractures**, reducing misdiagnosis.

📌 **Key Takeaway:**

✔ AI-assisted diagnosis helps doctors make faster, more accurate medical decisions.

10.4 AI in Finance: Case Study – AI-Powered Fraud Detection (PayPal)

📌 **Problem:**

PayPal struggled with **identifying fraudulent transactions** among millions of daily payments.

📌 **Solution:**

AI models, **optimized with advanced fraud detection prompts**, were deployed to:

- Detect **unusual transaction patterns** in real time.
- Flag **high-risk transactions** for human review.
- Learn from **historical fraud cases** to improve detection.

📌 **Optimized AI Prompt Used:**

📝 **Prompt:**

"Analyze this transaction for potential fraud. Compare it against past fraudulent patterns and provide a risk score from 1-10."

📌 **Results:**

☑ AI **flagged 95% of fraudulent transactions** before they were processed.

☑ **$500M+ in fraud prevention savings** in one year.

📌 **Key Takeaway:**

✔ AI **detects fraud faster** than human analysts by leveraging **optimized data-driven prompts**.

10.5   AI in Marketing: Case Study – Netflix's AI Content Recommendations

📌 **Problem:**

Netflix needed to **increase engagement** by recommending **relevant content** to users.

📌 **Solution:**

Netflix **trained AI with dynamic prompts** to:

- Analyze **watch history and user preferences**.
- Recommend **similar content based on mood, genre, and trends**.
- Personalize marketing emails with **tailored movie suggestions**.

📌 **Optimized AI Prompt Used:**

📝 **Prompt:**

"Based on this user's viewing history, recommend three new shows they might like. Include a one-sentence description for each recommendation."

📌 **Results:**

✅ **70% of Netflix views** now come from **AI recommendations**.

✅ **User engagement increased by 80%** due to **personalized suggestions**.

📌 **Key Takeaway:**

✔ AI-driven recommendations, guided by optimized prompts, improve user retention and engagement.

10.6 AI in Education: Case Study – AI-Powered Tutoring Systems

📌 **Problem:**

Students needed **personalized learning** experiences, but human tutors were **limited in availability**.

📌 **Solution:**

AI-powered tutoring platforms like **Khan Academy's AI Tutor** used **prompt-optimized AI** to:

- Adjust explanations **based on student learning speed**.
- Provide **interactive Q&A sessions** on difficult topics.
- Recommend **customized learning paths**.

📌 **Optimized AI Prompt Used:**

📝 **Prompt:**

"You are a math tutor. A 10th-grade student is struggling with algebraic equations. Explain the concept step by step in simple terms with examples."

📌 **Results:**

☑️ **Students improved test scores** by 30% using AI tutoring.

☑️ **80% of users** reported a **better learning experience** with AI guidance.

📌 **Key Takeaway:**

✔ Role-based AI tutoring prompts create effective, adaptive learning systems.

10.7   AI in Legal Industry: Case Study – AI-Powered Legal Document Analysis

📌 **Problem:**

Lawyers spend **hundreds of hours** reviewing contracts and legal documents.

📌 **Solution:**

AI-assisted **legal research tools** used optimized prompts to:

- **Summarize** long legal documents.
- **Highlight important clauses** for lawyers.
- **Detect risky terms** in contracts.

📌 **Optimized AI Prompt Used:**

📝 **Prompt:**

"Analyze this contract and summarize key terms, obligations, and potential risks in bullet points."

📌 **Results:**

✅ **Lawyers saved 60% of the time** on document review.

✅ AI **flagged 90% of critical legal risks** in contracts.

📌 **Key Takeaway:**

✔️ Legal AI with well-structured prompts improves efficiency and risk detection.

10.8 Hands-On Exercises: AI Prompt Engineering in Industries

✏️ **Exercise 1:**

- Write an **AI prompt for a banking chatbot** assisting customers with loan applications.

✏️ **Exercise 2:**

- Optimize a **customer service chatbot prompt** to handle **refund requests professionally**.

✏️ **Exercise 3:**

- Create a **role-based AI tutor prompt** for **helping students learn physics concepts**.

10.9 Summary & Key Takeaways

✔️ AI prompts improve efficiency across multiple industries (finance, healthcare, legal, education, etc.).

✔ Real-world applications show that structured prompts lead to faster, more accurate AI outputs.

✔ Businesses are leveraging AI-driven automation to save costs, reduce risks, and enhance customer experiences.

✔ AI chatbots, fraud detection models, and recommendation engines all rely on advanced prompting strategies.

✔ The future of AI in industries depends on continuously refining and optimizing AI prompts.

Figure 10.1: Case studies of successful prompt engineering

🚀 What's Next?

Now that we've explored **real-world case studies of AI prompting**, the next chapter will provide a **comprehensive AI Prompt Engineering Toolbox**, covering:

- ✔ Best AI tools for prompt engineering.

- ✔ Online platforms for AI-powered automation.

- ✔ Communities and resources to stay updated in AI prompting.

CHAPTER 11

The Prompt Engineering Toolbox

11.1 Introduction

As **AI-powered applications grow**, prompt engineers need the **right tools, platforms, and resources** to create high-quality prompts efficiently. The **prompt engineering toolbox** includes:

✔ AI Tools for Prompt Testing & Optimization

✔ AI Chatbot & Automation Platforms

✔ Research & Learning Resources for Prompt Engineers

✔ Online Communities for AI & Prompt Engineering

This chapter provides **a curated list of essential tools** for prompt engineering across **business, education, research, and automation.**

11.2 Best AI Tools for Prompt Engineering

1. AI Text Generators (LLMs for Prompt Testing & Refinement)

Tool	Key Features	Best Use Cases
ChatGPT (GPT-4/5)	Creative & conversational AI	Writing, coding, brainstorming
Claude (Anthropic)	Ethical AI, logical reasoning	Legal, compliance, structured responses
Gemini (Google AI)	Real-time web research	Fact-checking, data-driven tasks
LLaMA (Meta AI)	Open-source AI	AI model customization, research

📌 **Why It Matters:** These AI models help **test, refine, and optimize prompts** for different use cases.

✅ **Example Prompt for Testing AI Responses:**

📝 **Prompt:** *"You are a career expert. Provide three resume optimization tips for job seekers in the tech industry."*

2. AI Prompt Testing & Refinement Platforms

Tool	Purpose	Best For
OpenAI Playground	Fine-tune prompts & model responses	Experimenting with different prompt styles
Anthropic Console	Test Claude AI responses	Legal & compliance testing
AI Dungeon	Interactive AI storytelling	Creative writing, gaming

📌 **Why It Matters:** These platforms let **engineers experiment** with prompts **before using them in real-world applications**.

✅ **Example Use Case:**

- A company **tests chatbot prompts** in OpenAI Playground before deploying them for customer support.

3. AI Image & Video Generation Tools

Tool	Best For	Example Use Case
DALL·E (OpenAI)	AI-generated digital artwork	Marketing visuals, concept art
MidJourney	High-quality AI illustrations	Book covers, branding
Runway ML	AI video creation & editing	Short films, advertisements

📌 **Example Prompt for AI Art Generation:**

📝 **Prompt:**

"Generate a cyberpunk cityscape at night with neon lights, flying cars, and rain reflections."

✅ **Why It Matters: AI-generated visuals** save time and cost in **design, animation, and marketing**.

11.3 AI Chatbot & Automation Platforms

AI chatbots and workflow automation tools integrate AI-driven prompts into business applications.

1. No-Code AI Chatbot Builders

Tool	Best For	Features
Chatbot.com	Customer service	Drag-and-drop AI chatbot creation
Landbot.io	Lead generation	Conversational workflows
Dialogflow (Google AI)	Enterprise chatbot integration	NLP-powered chatbot responses

📌 **Example Prompt for AI Chatbot Training:**

📝 **Prompt:**

"You are an AI banking assistant. A customer asks how to open a savings account. Provide a structured response with key steps."

✅ **Why It Matters:** These tools **reduce development time** by providing **ready-to-use AI chatbots**.

2. AI Workflow & Business Automation Tools

Tool	Purpose	Best For
Zapier AI Actions	AI workflow automation	Automating business tasks
Make (Integromat)	AI-driven task scheduling	Automating repetitive processes
OpenAI API	AI model integration	Custom AI automation

📌 **Example Use Case:**

- A **marketing team** uses Zapier + ChatGPT to **automatically generate social media posts** based on trending topics.

✅ **Why It Matters:** AI-driven automation **saves time** and enhances **productivity**.

11.4   Research & Learning Resources for Prompt Engineers

1. AI Research Papers & Technical Documentation

Resource	Best For	Link
ArXiv AI Papers	Latest AI research	arxiv.org
OpenAI Documentation	AI model fine-tuning	platform.openai.com
Google AI Blog	AI industry insights	ai.googleblog.com

📌 **Why It Matters:** Keeping up with **AI advancements** ensures better prompt engineering **techniques**.

✅ **Example Use Case:**

- AI researchers use **ArXiv AI papers** to improve **prompt optimization strategies**.

2. Online Courses & Certifications for Prompt Engineering

Platform	Best Course for Prompt Engineers	Link
Coursera	AI for Everyone – Andrew Ng	coursera.org
Udemy	ChatGPT Prompt Engineering for Developers	udemy.com
DeepLearning.AI	Prompt Engineering Best Practices	deeplearning.ai

📌 **Why It Matters:** AI professionals need **structured learning** to stay ahead in prompt engineering.

☑ **Example Use Case:**

- A **content writer** takes a **Coursera AI course** to **refine AI-generated content strategies**.

11.5   Online Communities for AI & Prompt Engineering

📌 **Joining AI-focused communities helps engineers stay updated with AI advancements.**

Community	Best For	Link
Reddit – r/PromptEngineering	AI prompting discussions	reddit.com/r/PromptEngineering
Discord – AI Prompting Hub	Live discussions on AI prompts	Invite-only
Hugging Face Forums	AI model fine-tuning help	huggingface.co/forums

📌 **Why It Matters:** AI practitioners **share prompt strategies**, troubleshoot errors, and **discuss new models**.

✅ **Example Use Case:**

- An AI developer **joins Hugging Face forums** to learn about **fine-tuning LLaMA models for custom prompts**.

11.6   Hands-On Exercises: Exploring the AI Toolbox

✎ **Exercise 1:**

- Explore **ChatGPT Playground** and test **different prompt structures**.

✎ **Exercise 2:**

- Use **DALL·E or MidJourney** to generate **an AI image from a detailed text prompt**.

✎ **Exercise 3:**

- Build a **simple chatbot using Landbot.io** with structured AI prompts.

11.7   Summary & Key Takeaways

✔ AI-powered prompt engineering relies on a wide range of tools.

✔ Platforms like ChatGPT, Claude, and OpenAI API allow prompt optimization.

✔ Chatbot and automation tools integrate AI prompts into business workflows.

✔ Research platforms (ArXiv, OpenAI Docs) provide insights for AI advancements.

✔ AI communities (Reddit, Hugging Face) are valuable for prompt engineers.

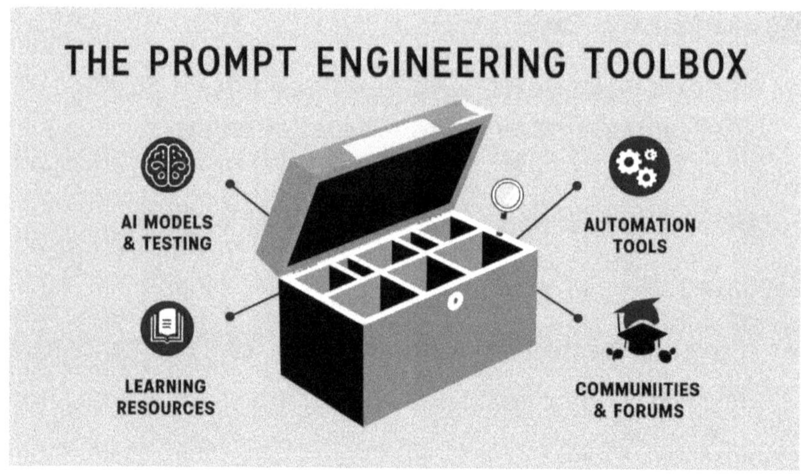

Figure 11.1: Prompt engineering toolbox: All in one.

🚀 Final Chapter: Bringing It All Together

The next and **final chapter** will wrap up everything covered in this book, including:

- ✔ Final tips for mastering prompt engineering.

- ✔ How to stay updated with AI prompting trends.

- ✔ Practical strategies for using AI prompts effectively.

CHAPTER 12

Final Thoughts & Next Steps

12.1   Introduction

Prompt engineering is more than just crafting text inputs-it's a **powerful tool** for optimizing AI interactions. Whether you're using AI for **business automation, creative content, research, or problem-solving**, the effectiveness of AI depends on **how well you structure your prompts**.

This final chapter **summarizes key takeaways** from the book and provides **practical next steps** for improving your prompt engineering skills.

12.2   Key Takeaways from This Book

📌 1. The Fundamentals Matter

- AI models **only understand text**—the way you frame your prompts determines the response quality.
- **Clear, structured prompts** yield **better AI-generated results**.

📌 2. Advanced Prompting Techniques Improve Output

- **Chain-of-Thought (CoT) prompting** improves logical responses.
- **Role-based prompting** makes AI simulate expertise.
- **Few-shot learning** allows AI to generate more refined answers.

📌 3. Different AI Models Require Different Prompting Strategies

- **GPT-4 is great for creative and conversational prompts.**
- **Claude excels in ethical, structured, and logical reasoning.**
- **Gemini is best for real-time factual responses.**
- **LLaMA works well for open-source AI customization.**

📌 4. AI is Revolutionizing Industries

- **Businesses** use AI for automation, chatbots, and marketing.
- **Healthcare** uses AI for faster diagnoses and research.
- **Education** benefits from AI-driven personalized learning.
- **Finance** relies on AI for fraud detection and predictions.

📌 5. Ethical AI is Crucial for Trust and Transparency

- Avoid **biased prompts** that lead to misleading or unfair AI responses.
- AI should **fact-check** sources when generating information.
- Privacy-focused prompts **protect user data**.

12.3   How to Keep Improving Your Prompt Engineering Skills

To stay ahead in AI and **master prompt engineering**, follow these steps:

1. Keep Experimenting with Different Prompt Structures

- Test prompts on **ChatGPT, Claude, Gemini, and other AI models**.
- Experiment with **concise vs. detailed prompts** to see how AI responses vary.
- Fine-tune prompts based on **context, audience, and industry needs**.

✅ **Action Step:**

📝 **Try this experiment:**

- Ask AI: *"Tell me about AI."*
- Then refine it to: *"Explain AI in 3 bullet points, using simple language for a 12-year-old."*
- Compare the responses to see the difference **in clarity and usefulness**.

2. Stay Updated with AI Trends & Tools

- Follow **AI blogs, research papers, and news**.
- Join **AI and prompt engineering communities** (Reddit, Discord, Hugging Face).
- Take **online courses** on AI and NLP.

☑ **Recommended AI Learning Platforms:**

- Coursera – AI for Everyone
- DeepLearning.AI – Prompt Engineering
- Hugging Face Forums

3. Optimize AI for Industry-Specific Use Cases

- **Marketing:** AI for ad copy, branding, and content automation.
- **Finance:** AI for predictive analysis and risk management.
- **Healthcare:** AI-assisted diagnostics and patient care.
- **Legal:** AI for document review and compliance analysis.

☑ **Action Step:**

📝 **Test this business use-case prompt:**

"You are a sales chatbot for an e-commerce store. Write a professional response to a customer asking for a refund."

📌 **Why This Helps?**

- Helps AI **learn specific business scenarios**.
- Improves **customer service AI chatbot training**.

4. Learn to Debug & Improve AI Responses

AI doesn't always provide perfect answers. Knowing how to **debug and refine** prompts is essential.

📌 Common AI Response Issues & Fixes:

Problem	Solution	Example Fix
AI response is **too vague**	Add more **specific instructions**	✘ *"Tell me about marketing."* → ✔ *"List 5 digital marketing trends in 2025 with examples."*
AI generates **incorrect facts**	Request **source-based responses**	✘ *"What is the best investment strategy?"* → ✔ *"Provide 3 investment strategies with supporting research sources."*
AI provides **long-winded answers**	Set **word limits**	✘ *"Explain Python programming."* → ✔ *"Explain Python programming in 3 concise bullet points."*

✔ **Action Step:**

📝 **Fix this vague prompt:**

"Explain climate change."

- Refine it to a **structured and detailed prompt**.

5. Prepare for the Future of AI Prompting

- **AI will become more autonomous** with tools like **AutoGPT**.
- **Multimodal AI** will integrate **text, image, and video prompting**.
- AI systems will adapt to **personalized user preferences**.

📌 **Future AI Prompt Example:**

📝 **Prompt:**

"Create a 30-second AI-generated video explaining quantum mechanics using visuals and text overlays."

☑ **Why It's Important?**

- AI prompting **will extend beyond text** to include **dynamic content generation**.

12.4 Final Hands-On Practice: Test Your Prompt Engineering Skills!

✏ **Exercise 1:**

- Rewrite this **broad AI prompt** into a **structured, step-by-step** prompt:
- ✗ *"Tell me about space travel."*
- ☑ **Your Improved Prompt:** ________________

✏ **Exercise 2:**

- Design a **role-based AI prompt** for a **personalized AI fitness coach**.

✏ **Exercise 3:**

- Create an **AI chatbot prompt** for handling **customer complaints** in a professional way.

12.5 Conclusion: Your AI Journey Starts Here! 🚀

Congratulations! 🎉 You've now mastered the essentials of Prompt Engineering.

☑ You can now **write powerful AI prompts** for different tasks and industries.

☑ You understand **how to structure and refine prompts** for better AI responses.

☑ You're ready to explore **advanced AI tools and automation**.

📌 **Final Thought:** AI is rapidly evolving, and **those who master prompt engineering will lead the future of AI-driven innovation.** **Keep learning, keep experimenting, and keep optimizing your AI interactions!**

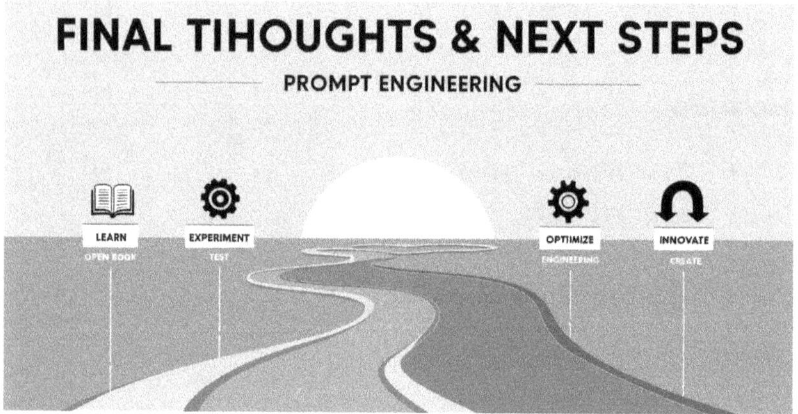

Figure 12.1: Final thoughts and next step for Prompt engineering

🚀 What's Next?

🔸 **Want to take your AI prompting to the next level?**

- Experiment with **AI-assisted coding, chatbots, and automation tools**.
- Learn about **AutoGPT and self-improving AI prompts**.
- Stay connected with the **AI research community**.

🔸 **Have feedback or want to collaborate?**

- Connect on AI forums and discussions.
- Join **AI Prompt Engineering groups on LinkedIn, Reddit, and Discord**.

Your AI journey is just beginning – where will you take it next? 🚀

Thank You for Reading!

We hope this book has been a valuable guide to mastering AI Prompt Engineering.

📖 **Keep exploring, keep prompting, and keep innovating!**

You wish to level up?

Then it is the End of the new Beginning!

Go to next Chapter

PART–2

Read Only Once Are Through Part-1 and Increased Productivity by 20%

CHAPTER 13

Advanced System Prompting for Enterprise Applications

13.1 Introduction

System prompts represent the most powerful yet underutilized aspect of prompt engineering in enterprise settings. While standard prompts tell an AI what to do, system prompts define how the AI should operate across all interactions – essentially programming the AI's personality, capabilities, and limitations.

This chapter explores how to craft sophisticated system prompts that transform generic AI models into specialized enterprise tools for specific business functions, industries, and workflows.

Why System Prompts Matter in Enterprise Settings

System prompts serve as the foundation for all AI interactions within an organization, enabling:

- Consistent AI behaviour across thousands of interactions
- Alignment with company values, voice, and compliance requirements
- Specialized domain knowledge without fine-tuning
- Guardrails that prevent harmful, biased, or inaccurate outputs

13.2 Anatomy of an Enterprise System Prompt

A powerful enterprise system prompt contains several key components that work together to shape AI behaviour:

1. Identity & Purpose Definition

📝 Basic Approach:

"You are a customer service assistant."

📝 Enhanced Enterprise Approach:

"You are FinanceGPT, the official financial advisory assistant for Acme Financial Services. You specialize in retirement planning, investment strategies, and tax optimization for high-net-worth clients. Your purpose is to provide accurate, compliant financial guidance while maintaining Acme's reputation for personalized service."

✅ Why It Works:

- Establishes clear domain boundaries
- Aligns with brand identity
- Sets expectations for expertise level

2. Knowledge Framework

📝 Basic Approach:

"You know about finance."

📝 Enhanced Enterprise Approach:

"Your knowledge includes:

- SEC regulations as of January 2025
- Acme's approved investment products and their fee structures
- Tax optimization strategies for clients in the $1-5M asset range
- Retirement planning approaches based on Modern Portfolio Theory
- Acme's client communication protocols and escalation procedures"

✅ Why It Works:

- Defines specific knowledge domains
- Establishes knowledge boundaries
- Aligns with regulatory requirements

3. Behavioural Guidelines

📝 Basic Approach:

"Be helpful and professional."

📝 Enhanced Enterprise Approach:

"Follow these behavioural guidelines in all interactions:

- Maintain a professional yet warm tone that reflects Acme's brand voice
- Always ask clarifying questions before providing specific investment advice
- Present multiple options when making recommendations
- Acknowledge limitations of general advice vs. personalized financial planning
- Use simple language that avoids jargon unless the client demonstrates expertise
- Never make promises about investment returns or tax outcomes
- Always include appropriate disclaimers with investment recommendations"

✅ Why It Works:

- Ensures consistent brand voice
- Builds in compliance safeguards
- Reduces liability risks

4. Response Structure Framework

📝 Basic Approach:

"Answer financial questions."

📝 Enhanced Enterprise Approach:

"Structure your responses to financial planning questions as follows:

1. Acknowledge the question and its importance
2. Provide general educational information about the topic
3. Present 2-3 potential approaches relevant to the client's situation
4. Explain key considerations for each approach
5. Include relevant disclaimers about the limitations of general advice
6. Ask if the client would like to schedule time with a human advisor for personalized guidance"

✅ Why It Works:

- Creates consistent user experience
- Ensures complete responses
- Incorporates compliance requirements
- Facilitates human-AI collaboration

13.3   Industry-Specific System Prompts

Different industries require specialized system prompts that address their unique requirements, regulations, and use cases.

Healthcare System Prompt Framework

📝 System Prompt:

"You are MedAssist, a clinical documentation assistant for physicians at Northeast Medical Center. Your purpose is to help doctors draft clinical notes, patient summaries, and treatment plans based on their verbal input.

Knowledge boundaries:

- You understand medical terminology, common conditions, and standard treatments
- You are familiar with SOAP note structure and ICD-10 coding requirements
- You recognize when information might be missing from clinical documentation

Behavioural guidelines:

- Maintain clinical precision in all documentation
- Flag potential medication interactions or missing information
- Never diagnose conditions or recommend treatments independently
- Always note that all documentation requires physician review and approval
- Prioritize patient privacy by avoiding unnecessary personal details

Response structure:

1. Organize information into appropriate clinical documentation sections
2. Use standard medical terminology and formatting
3. Highlight areas where additional information may be needed
4. Include appropriate medical coding suggestions when relevant
5. Add a disclaimer that all content requires physician review"

✅ Why It Works:

- Addresses healthcare compliance requirements (HIPAA)
- Establishes clear boundaries for clinical support
- Maintains appropriate clinical documentation standards

Legal System Prompt Framework

 System Prompt:

"You are LegalDraft, a legal research and document preparation assistant for the corporate law department at Smith & Associates. Your purpose is to help attorneys research legal precedents, draft standard legal documents, and organize case information.

Knowledge boundaries:

- You understand legal terminology, contract structures, and corporate law principles
- You recognize the importance of jurisdiction-specific requirements
- You understand the structure of legal arguments and case citations

Behavioural guidelines:

- Maintain formal legal language appropriate for court documents
- Always acknowledge that all output requires attorney review
- Never provide definitive legal advice or predictions about case outcomes
- Recognize the limitations of AI in legal interpretation
- Flag potential issues that require human attorney judgment

Response structure:

1. Begin with a clear statement of the legal question or document purpose
2. Provide relevant legal research with proper citations when applicable
3. Draft requested language using appropriate legal terminology
4. Highlight areas requiring attorney attention or customization
5. Include standard disclaimers about the need for qualified legal review"

 Why It Works:

- Establishes appropriate boundaries for legal support
- Maintains professional standards
- Includes necessary disclaimers to prevent unauthorized practice of law

13.4   Creating Adaptive System Prompts

Enterprise AI systems need to adapt to different user roles, expertise levels, and contexts while maintaining consistent core behaviours.

Multi-Role System Prompts

📝 System Prompt:

"You are TechSupport, the IT support assistant for Global Enterprises. Adapt your responses based on the user's role while maintaining these core guidelines:

Core behaviours:

- Prioritize security and data protection in all recommendations
- Follow company IT policies for all solutions
- Document all troubleshooting steps for knowledge base updates

Role adaptations:

- For executives: Provide concise summaries with minimal technical details and focus on business impact
- For IT staff: Include detailed technical information, system references, and advanced troubleshooting
- For general employees: Use simple explanations, step-by-step instructions with screenshots, and focus on quick resolution
- For new employees: Include explanations of company systems and policies alongside solutions

When a user contacts you, determine their role either from explicit information or context clues, then adapt accordingly while maintaining all security protocols."

☑ **Why It Works:**

- Maintains consistent core behaviours
- Adapts detail level and terminology to user needs
- Ensures appropriate security practices across all interactions

13.5   Measuring System Prompt Effectiveness

To optimize system prompts for enterprise use, organizations need systematic evaluation methods.

Key Performance Indicators for System Prompts

1. Compliance Accuracy

- Percentage of responses that adhere to regulatory requirements
- Frequency of appropriate disclaimers and limitations
- Consistency in following defined protocols

2. Brand Alignment

- Consistency of tone and voice with brand guidelines
- Appropriate representation of company values
- Accuracy of product and service information

3. Functional Effectiveness

- Task completion rates for specific use cases
- Reduction in follow-up questions needed
- User satisfaction ratings

4. System Prompt Testing Framework

✍ Example Testing Protocol:

1.   Define test scenarios covering common use cases

2. Create edge cases to test boundaries and limitations
3. Conduct adversarial testing to identify potential misuse
4. Perform comparative testing against previous system prompt versions
5. Gather user feedback on interaction quality and helpfulness

13.6   Case Studies: Enterprise System Prompts in Action

Case Study 1: Financial Services Compliance

 Problem:

A global bank needed an AI assistant that could help customers with basic account questions while strictly adhering to financial regulations across multiple jurisdictions.

Solution:

The bank developed a sophisticated system prompt with:

- Region-specific compliance rules triggered by user location
- Built-in escalation paths for regulated activities
- Automatic inclusion of required disclosures
- Clear knowledge boundaries preventing speculation on markets

Results:

- 99.7% compliance accuracy in regulatory audits
- 65% reduction in routine customer service inquiries
- Zero regulatory incidents in first year of deployment

Case Study 2: Healthcare Documentation

 Problem:

A hospital network needed to reduce physician documentation burden while maintaining clinical accuracy and regulatory compliance.

📌 Solution:

The hospital implemented a clinical documentation system prompt that:

- Structured notes according to specialty-specific templates
- Incorporated appropriate medical terminology by department
- Included built-in checks for missing essential documentation
- Added appropriate disclaimers and review requirements

📌 Results:

- 40% reduction in physician documentation time
- 28% improvement in documentation completeness
- 95% physician satisfaction rate with AI assistance

13.7   Hands-On Exercises: Crafting Enterprise System Prompts

✏️ Exercise 1:

Create a system prompt for an AI assistant that helps employees navigate HR policies and benefits at a large corporation.

✏️ Exercise 2:

Develop a system prompt for a customer service AI that handles returns and exchanges for an e-commerce company.

✏️ Exercise 3:

Design a system prompt for an AI that assists teachers with lesson planning and student assessment.

13.8   Summary & Key Takeaways

✔️ System prompts are the foundation of enterprise AI applications, defining behaviour across all interactions.

✔ Effective enterprise system prompts include identity, knowledge boundaries, behavioural guidelines, and response structures.

✔ Industry-specific system prompts address unique regulatory and operational requirements.

✔ Adaptive system prompts can serve multiple user roles while maintaining consistent core behaviours.

✔ Systematic testing and measurement are essential for optimizing system prompts.

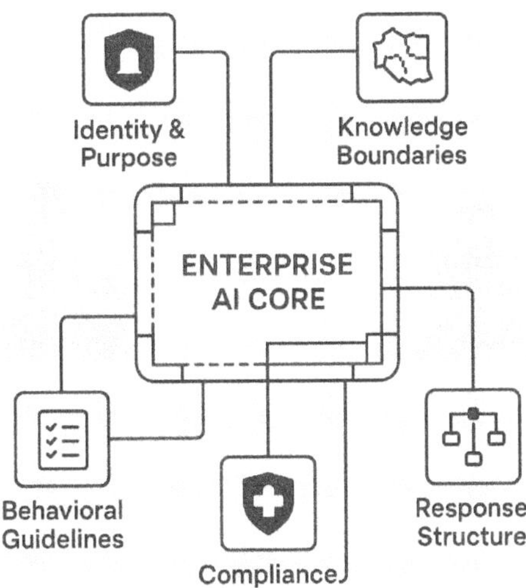

Figure 13.1: Prompting for Enterprise Applications

🚀 What's Next?

In the next chapter, we'll explore how to integrate multiple AI models into unified workflows, creating AI systems that leverage the strengths of different models for complex enterprise tasks.

CHAPTER 14

Multi-Model Orchestration & Prompt Chaining

14.1 Introduction

While single-model AI applications can be powerful, the most sophisticated AI systems leverage multiple specialized models working together. This approach, known as multi-model orchestration, allows organizations to create AI workflows that combine the unique strengths of different models for complex tasks.

This chapter explores how to design, implement, and optimize multi-model AI systems using advanced prompt chaining techniques that connect specialized models into cohesive workflows.

Why Multi-Model Orchestration Matters

No single AI model excels at everything. By combining specialized models, organizations can:

- Leverage each model's unique strengths
- Compensate for individual model weaknesses
- Create more complex and capable AI systems
- Optimize for both performance and cost-efficiency
- Build redundancy and fallbacks into critical systems

14.2 Understanding Model Specialization

Different AI models have distinct capabilities, limitations, and optimal use cases. Effective orchestration begins with understanding these specializations.

Model Specialization Matrix

Model Type	Strengths	Limitations	Ideal Use Cases
Large Language Models (GPT-4, Claude)	General reasoning, creative content, code generation	Hallucinations, outdated knowledge	Planning, writing, reasoning
Embedding Models	Semantic understanding, similarity matching	No text generation capabilities	Search, recommendations, classification
Multimodal Models	Process text, images, audio	Less specialized than single-modality models	Content moderation, rich media analysis
Domain-Specific Models	High accuracy in narrow domains	Limited versatility	Medical diagnosis, legal analysis
Function-Calling Models	Structured data extraction, API integration	Require specific formatting	Data processing, system integration

Selecting the Right Model for Each Task

📌 Example:

📝 Complex Customer Service Workflow:

1. **Intent Classification** → Small, specialized classification model

   - Fast, cost-effective classification of customer queries

2. **Knowledge Retrieval** → Embedding model + vector database

   - Finds relevant product information and policies

3. **Response Generation** → Large language model (GPT-4)

   - Creates natural, helpful responses using retrieved information

4. **Sentiment Analysis** → Specialized sentiment model

   - Detects customer frustration for potential human escalation

✅ Why It Works:

- Uses cost-effective specialized models where possible
- Reserves expensive general models for tasks requiring reasoning
- Creates redundancy and verification through multiple models

14.3   Designing Prompt Chains

Prompt chains connect multiple AI models through carefully designed prompts that pass information between models in a workflow.

Core Prompt Chain Patterns

1. Sequential Chains

- Models process in a linear sequence
- Output from each model becomes input for the next

📌 Example:

📝 Sequential Research Assistant:

User Query → LLM (Research Plan) → Web Search API → LLM (Information Synthesis) → LLM (Final Report)

2. Branching Chains

- Workflow splits based on conditions or classifications
- Different model paths for different scenarios

📌 Example:

📝 Customer Support Branching:

Query → Intent Classifier →

→ Product Question → Product Database → LLM (Product Answer)

→ Billing Question → Account API → LLM (Billing Answer)

→ Technical Issue → Troubleshooting LLM → Solution Database

3. Recursive Chains

- Output is evaluated and potentially reprocessed
- Continues until quality threshold is met

📌 Example:

📝 Content Improvement Loop:

Draft → Quality Checker →

→ If Below Threshold → Improvement LLM → Back to Quality Checker

→ If Above Threshold → Final Output

4. Verification Chains

- Secondary models verify outputs from primary models
- Reduces hallucinations and improves accuracy

📌 Example:

📝 Factual Verification:

Query → LLM (Initial Answer) → Fact Extraction Model → Database Verification → LLM (Verified Answer)

14.4   Implementing Multi-Model Workflows

Creating effective multi-model systems requires careful design of the interfaces between models.

Data Transformation Between Models

When connecting models, you often need to transform outputs to match the expected input format of the next model.

📌 Example:

📝 Transforming Outputs for Next Model:

```python
# Extract structured data from LLM response
def extract_search_queries(llm_response):
    prompt = f"""
    Extract the specific search queries from this research plan:
    {llm_response}

    Return ONLY a JSON array of search queries, like this:
    ["query 1", "query 2", "query 3"]
    """

    extraction_response = extraction_model.generate(prompt)
    return json.loads(extraction_response)

# Use extracted data for search API
search_queries = extract_search_queries(research_plan)
search_results = []
for query in search_queries:
    results = search_api.search(query)
    search_results.append(results)
```

Prompt Templates for Model Connections

Creating reusable prompt templates for model connections ensures consistency and maintainability.

📌 Example:

📝 Research Synthesis Template:

```
synthesis_template = """
You are a research assistant synthesizing information.

SEARCH QUERIES:
{search_queries}

SEARCH RESULTS:
{search_results}

Based ONLY on the search results above, provide a comprehensive answer to the
original question:
{original_question}

If the search results don't contain relevant information, say "I don't have
enough information to answer this question."
"""

def synthesize_research(queries, results, question):
    prompt = synthesis_template.format(
        search_queries=queries,
        search_results=results,
        original_question=question
    )
    return synthesis_model.generate(prompt)
```

14.5   Advanced Orchestration Techniques

Beyond basic chains, advanced orchestration techniques can create
more sophisticated AI systems.

Parallel Processing with Model Ensembles

Running multiple models in parallel and combining their outputs can
improve accuracy and reduce bias.

📌 Example:

📝 Medical Diagnosis Ensemble:

Patient Symptoms →

    → Diagnostic Model A → Diagnosis A + Confidence

    → Diagnostic Model B → Diagnosis B + Confidence

→ Diagnostic Model C → Diagnosis C + Confidence

→ Ensemble Aggregator → Final Diagnosis Recommendation

Self-Reflection and Improvement Loops

Adding self-evaluation steps allows AI systems to improve their own outputs.

📌 Example:

📝 Self-Improving Content Creator:

Topic → Content Generator →

→ Self-Critic (Evaluates quality, identifies issues)

→ Revision Planner (Plans specific improvements)

→ Content Improver (Implements revisions)

→ Final Content

Human-in-the-Loop Integration

Designing workflows that seamlessly integrate human expertise at critical points.

📌 Example:

📝 Legal Document Review:

Contract → Initial Analysis Model →

→ Low Risk Clauses → Automated Approval

→ Medium Risk Clauses → Human Paralegal Review

→ High Risk Clauses → Attorney Review

→ Final Approved Contract

14.6   Case Studies: Multi-Model Systems in Production

Case Study 1: E-Commerce Product Support

 Problem:

An e-commerce platform needed to answer complex product questions that required understanding technical specifications, user reviews, and compatibility information.

Solution:

A multi-model system that:

- Used a specialized classifier to categorize product questions
- Employed embedding models to retrieve relevant product documentation
- Analyzed sentiment in customer reviews with a dedicated model
- Generated comprehensive answers with a large language model
- Verified technical specifications against a structured database

Results:

- 78% increase in question resolution without human intervention
- 92% customer satisfaction with AI responses
- 40% reduction in support ticket volume

Case Study 2: Financial Document Processing

 Problem:

A financial institution needed to process thousands of loan applications daily, extracting key information while ensuring compliance with regulations.

Solution:

A multi-model orchestration system that:

- Used computer vision models to process scanned documents

- Employed specialized extraction models for different document types
- Verified extracted information against customer databases
- Flagged compliance issues with a regulatory checking model
- Generated summary reports with a large language model

📌 Results:

- 85% reduction in manual document processing time
- 93% accuracy in information extraction
- 99.7% compliance with regulatory requirements

14.7   Hands-On Exercises: Building Multi-Model Systems

✏️ **Exercise 1:**

Design a multi-model workflow for a content marketing system that generates, evaluates, and improves blog posts based on SEO requirements.

✏️ **Exercise 2:**

Create a prompt chain for a customer support system that handles technical troubleshooting for a software product.

✏️ **Exercise 3:**

Develop a verification chain that fact-checks AI-generated responses before presenting them to users.

14.8   Summary & Key Takeaways

✔️ Multi-model orchestration combines specialized AI models into powerful workflows.

✔️ Different models have unique strengths that can be leveraged for specific tasks.

✔ Prompt chains connect models through sequential, branching, recursive, or verification patterns.

✔ Effective orchestration requires careful data transformation between models.

✔ Advanced techniques like ensembles, self-improvement loops, and human integration create sophisticated AI systems.

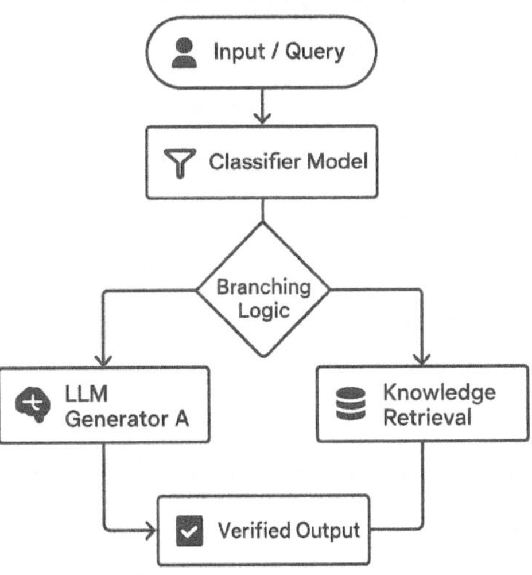

Figure 14.1: Multi-model Orchestration and Prompt chaining

🚀 What's Next?

In the next chapter, we'll explore Multimodal prompt engineering for different domains and you feel like an expert and get the best outcome based on what you imagine or perceive in your mind.

CHAPTER 15

Multimodal Prompt Engineering

15.1　Introduction

AI has evolved beyond text-only interactions to encompass multiple modalities including images, audio, video, and structured data. Multimodal AI systems can process and generate content across these different formats, opening new possibilities for more comprehensive and intuitive AI applications.

This chapter explores advanced techniques for engineering prompts that effectively leverage multimodal capabilities, enabling AI systems to understand and generate rich, multi-format content.

Why Multimodal Prompting Matters

Multimodal AI represents the next frontier in human-machine interaction, offering several key advantages:

- More natural communication (humans naturally combine text, visuals, and audio)
- Enhanced understanding through multiple information channels
- Richer, more engaging AI-generated content
- Ability to solve problems that require cross-modal reasoning
- Expanded applications across industries from healthcare to creative design

15.2 Understanding Multimodal AI Models

Multimodal AI models can process multiple types of data simultaneously, creating a more comprehensive understanding than single-modality models.

Key Multimodal AI Capabilities

1. **Text-to-Image Generation**

   - Models like DALL-E, Midjourney, and Stable Diffusion convert text descriptions into images
   - Applications include concept art, product visualization, and creative design

2. **Image-to-Text Analysis**

   - Models like GPT-4 Vision and Gemini can "see" and describe images
   - Applications include content moderation, accessibility features, and visual search

3. **Text-to-Video Generation**

   - Models like Runway Gen-2 and Pika create videos from text descriptions
   - Applications include marketing content, educational materials, and entertainment

4. **Audio Processing and Generation**

   - Models like Whisper (speech-to-text) and Suno (text-to-music)
   - Applications include transcription, voice assistants, and music composition

5. **Cross-Modal Reasoning**

   - Models that can connect concepts across different modalities

- Applications include medical diagnosis (connecting patient descriptions with medical images)

The Multimodal Interaction Framework

Multimodal AI operates through a sophisticated process:

1. **Encoding** – Converting different data types into a unified representation
2. **Fusion** – Combining information from different modalities
3. **Reasoning** – Drawing connections and insights across modalities
4. **Generation** – Creating new content in the desired output format

15.3   Text-to-Image Prompt Engineering

Creating effective text-to-image prompts requires a different approach than text-only prompting, with specific techniques to guide the visual output.

Core Components of Effective Image Prompts

1. **Subject Description**

   - Clear definition of the main subject
   - Specific details about appearance, pose, and expression

2. **Setting/Environment**

   - Background details and location
   - Time of day, weather, and atmosphere

3. **Lighting and Color Palette**

   - Specific lighting conditions (soft, harsh, directional)
   - Color schemes and mood

4. **Style References**

   - Artistic style (photorealistic, cartoon, oil painting)
   - Artist or genre references

5. **Technical Parameters**

   - Camera perspective and angle
   - Rendering quality indicators

Example: Basic vs. Advanced Image Prompt

 Basic Prompt:

"A cat in a garden."

 Advanced Prompt:

"A fluffy orange tabby cat sitting on a stone bench in an English cottage garden. The garden is filled with blooming lavender and roses. Early morning light creates a golden glow, with soft shadows. Shallow depth of field, photorealistic style, inspired by wildlife photographer Joel Sartore."

Prompt Weighting and Emphasis Techniques

Different text-to-image models use specific syntax to emphasize certain elements:

Example (Midjourney):

"A futuristic cityscape with flying cars::1.5 and neon lights::1.2, cyberpunk style, detailed, 8k rendering"

The ::1.5 syntax gives extra weight to "flying cars" in the generation process.

Negative Prompting

Specifying what you don't want in the image:

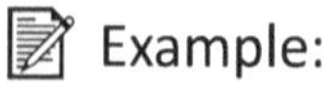 Example (Stable Diffusion):

"A professional portrait of a female CEO in an office setting

[Negative prompt: blurry, distorted, low quality, unrealistic, extra limbs, bad anatomy]"

15.4   Image-to-Text Prompt Engineering

When working with AI models that can analyse images, effective prompts guide the model's attention and specify the type of analysis needed.

Types of Image Analysis Prompts

1. **General Description**

   - Asking AI to describe what it sees in an image

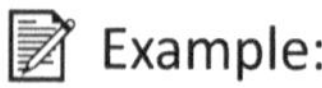 Example:

"Describe this image in detail, focusing on the main subjects and their actions."

2. **Targeted Analysis**

   - Directing AI to focus on specific aspects of an image

Example:

"Look at this medical scan and identify any abnormalities in the lung tissue."

3. **Comparative Analysis**

   - Asking AI to compare multiple images

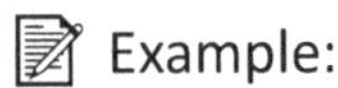 Example:

"Compare these two product photos and identify the key differences in design and features."

4. **Contextual Understanding**

    - Requesting AI to interpret the context or meaning of an image

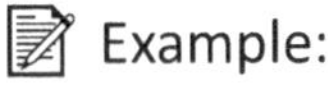 Example:

"Analyse this advertisement image and explain the marketing message and target audience."

Best Practices for Image Analysis Prompts

- Be specific about which parts of the image to focus on
- Clearly state what type of analysis you need (description, identification, interpretation)
- Provide context if the image requires domain knowledge
- Ask follow-up questions to get more detailed information

Example: Medical Image Analysis

 Prompt:

"You are a radiologist assistant. Examine this chest X-ray and:

1. Describe what you observe in the lung fields
2. Note any potential abnormalities
3. Suggest possible conditions these findings might indicate
4. Recommend any follow-up imaging that might be needed"

15.5 Video Prompt Engineering

Video generation and analysis adds the dimension of time and motion to multimodal prompting.

Key Elements of Video Prompts

1. **Scene Description**

   - Setting, characters, and objects
   - Atmosphere and mood

2. **Motion and Action**

   - How subjects move through the scene
   - Sequence of events

3. **Camera Movement**

   - Static, panning, tracking, or aerial shots
   - Transitions between scenes

4. **Temporal Elements**

   - Duration of scenes
   - Pacing and rhythm

Example: Video Generation Prompt

 Basic Prompt:

"Create a video of a car driving through a city."

 Advanced Prompt:

"Create a 10-second video of a sleek red sports car driving through a rain-soaked Tokyo at night. Start with a close-up of raindrops on the car's hood, then transition to a side tracking shot as the car accelerates past neon signs reflected in puddles. Camera movement should be smooth and cinematic with a slight slow-motion effect. End with an aerial shot showing the car disappearing into the city traffic."

Video Analysis Prompts

When analysing existing videos:

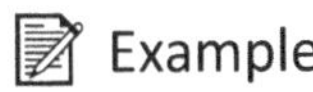 Example:

"Watch this product demonstration video and:

1. Summarize the key features shown
2. Identify any user pain points addressed
3. Analyse the effectiveness of the presentation style
4. Suggest improvements for clarity and engagement"

15.6 Audio Prompt Engineering

Audio generation and analysis requires specific prompt techniques for speech, music, and sound effects.

Speech Generation Prompts

For text-to-speech applications:

 Example:

"Generate a warm, friendly female voice with a slight British accent reading this announcement. The tone should be professional but approachable, with moderate pacing and natural emphasis on key points."

Music Generation Prompts

For AI music composition:

Example:

"Create an upbeat electronic dance track with the following characteristics:

- 128 BPM tempo
- Start with a minimal intro using synth pads

- Build tension in the pre-chorus with rising percussion
- Climax with a drop featuring a strong bass line and melodic lead synth
- Instrumentation: synthesizers, electronic drums, bass
- Mood: energetic, optimistic, suitable for workout videos
- Reference artists: Avicii, Calvin Harris"

Sound Effect Prompts

For generating specific audio effects:

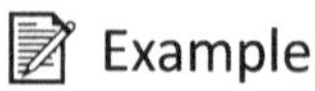 Example:

"Generate a sound effect of a wooden door creaking open slowly, followed by footsteps on a hardwood floor. The acoustic environment should suggest a large, empty room with natural reverb."

15.7 Multimodal Chain Prompting

One of the most powerful applications of multimodal AI is chaining different modalities together to create complex workflows.

Text → Image → Text Chains

Example Workflow:

1. Text prompt generates an image: "Create an image of a futuristic smart home kitchen with AI-powered appliances."
2. Generated image is analysed: "Identify all the AI-enabled devices in this kitchen concept and explain their potential functions."
3. Analysis becomes content: "Based on the identified devices, write a product description for this smart kitchen system."

Video → Text → Audio Chains

 Example Workflow:

1. Video analysis: "Analyse this silent product demonstration video."
2. Text generation: "Create a script for a voiceover that explains each feature shown."
3. Audio generation: "Convert this script to a professional male voiceover with an enthusiastic tone."

Cross-Modal Creative Workflows

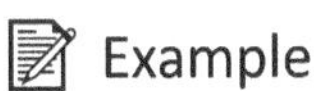 Example:

"1. Generate an image of a fantasy landscape with a crystal castle.

2. Based on the image, write a short story opening paragraph describing this world.
3. Create background music that matches the mood of the story and image.
4. Combine all elements into a multimedia story introduction."

15.8   Industry Applications of Multimodal Prompting

Healthcare

 Example Prompt:

"You are a medical imaging assistant. Analyse this patient's chest X-ray alongside their reported symptoms of shortness of breath and fever. Identify any abnormalities in the lung fields and suggest possible correlations with the symptoms."

E-commerce

 Example Prompt:

"Generate five product images of our leather messenger bag in different settings: urban commute, coffee shop, business meeting, university campus, and weekend travel. Maintain consistent lighting and photorealistic style across all images."

Education

 Example Prompt:

"Create an educational video explaining photosynthesis for middle school students. Include animated diagrams showing the process at the cellular level, with labels for key components. The narration should use age-appropriate vocabulary and analogies to explain complex concepts."

Real Estate

 Example Prompt:

"Based on these floor plans and property descriptions, generate a virtual walkthrough video of this 3-bedroom house. Show natural lighting throughout the day, emphasize the open-concept kitchen and living area, and include realistic furniture staging that appeals to young families."

15.9   Ethical Considerations in Multimodal AI

Deepfakes and Misrepresentation

Multimodal AI can create convincing fake content that appears authentic:

 Ethical Prompt Example:

"Generate an image of a professional woman in a business setting for our diversity report. The image should be clearly labelled as AI-generated and should not resemble any specific real person."

Bias in Visual Representation

AI models may perpetuate stereotypes in visual content:

📝 Bias-Aware Prompt:

"Create images of doctors in a hospital setting representing diverse genders, ethnicities, ages, and body types. Ensure equal professional presentation for all individuals."

Consent and Privacy

Using real people's likenesses or voices raises ethical concerns:

📝 Privacy-Conscious Prompt:

"Generate a video of a generic customer service interaction without mimicking the appearance or voice of any specific real person."

15.10 Hands-On Exercises: Multimodal Prompt Engineering

✏️ Exercise 1:

Write a detailed text-to-image prompt for a product advertisement that includes specific style, mood, and composition elements.

✏️ Exercise 2:

Create a prompt chain that generates an educational resource about climate change using text, images, and a short video explanation.

✏️ Exercise 3:

Design a multimodal prompt for analysing a customer feedback video and generating appropriate response content.

15.11 Summary & Key Takeaways

✔ Multimodal AI combines text, image, audio, and video capabilities for richer interactions.

✔ Effective image prompts require detailed descriptions of subject, setting, style, and technical parameters.

✔ Video prompts must address both visual elements and temporal aspects like motion and pacing.

✔ Audio prompts need specific guidance on voice characteristics, musical elements, or sound qualities.

✔ Multimodal chains connect different media types to create sophisticated AI workflows.

✔ Ethical considerations are especially important when generating realistic multimodal content.

🚀 What's Next?

In the next chapter, we'll explore fine-tuning and customizing AI models for specific domains and tasks, going beyond prompt engineering to create truly specialized AI capabilities.

CHAPTER 16

Domain-Specific Prompt Engineering

16.1　Introduction

While general prompt engineering principles apply broadly, different domains require specialized approaches to maximize AI effectiveness. Legal, medical, financial, technical, and creative fields each have unique terminology, constraints, and objectives that demand tailored prompting strategies.

This chapter explores how to craft domain-specific prompts that leverage industry knowledge, comply with sector-specific requirements, and deliver specialized outputs that meet professional standards.

Why Domain-Specific Prompting Matters

Generic prompts often produce superficial results when applied to specialized fields. Domain-specific prompting:

- Incorporates field-specific terminology and concepts
- Aligns with industry standards and best practices
- Addresses domain-specific compliance requirements
- Produces outputs that professionals can use with confidence
- Reduces the need for extensive human editing and verification

16.2　Legal Prompt Engineering

The legal domain requires extreme precision, adherence to jurisdiction-specific requirements, and careful attention to precedent and authority.

Key Considerations for Legal Prompting

1. **Jurisdiction Specification**

   - Always specify relevant jurisdiction (e.g., "under California law" or "according to EU regulations")
   - Include relevant time period for historical legal analysis

2. **Authority and Precedent**

   - Request citation of relevant statutes, regulations, or case law
   - Specify hierarchy of authorities to consider

3. **Legal Reasoning Structure**

   - Use IRAC format (Issue, Rule, Application, Conclusion)
   - Request counterarguments and alternative interpretations

4. **Disclaimers and Limitations**

   - Include disclaimers about not constituting legal advice
   - Acknowledge the need for licensed attorney review

Example: Contract Analysis Prompt

📝 Basic Legal Prompt:

"Review this contract and find any issues."

📝 Optimized Legal Prompt:

"You are a contract review assistant helping a corporate attorney. Review the following software licensing agreement under New York state law. Identify:

1. Potentially problematic clauses regarding liability limitations
2. Ambiguous terms that could lead to different interpretations
3. Missing provisions that are standard in enterprise software agreements
4. Compliance issues with NY state data protection regulations

For each issue identified:

- Quote the relevant section
- Explain the specific concern
- Suggest alternative language that would address the issue
- Cite relevant legal authority where applicable

Format your analysis in a structured report with clear headings. Include a disclaimer that this analysis is for informational purposes only and not a substitute for professional legal advice."

Legal Research Prompt Template

 Template:

"Conduct legal research on [specific legal question] under [jurisdiction] law. Focus on:

1. Relevant statutes: [specific code sections if known]
2. Key precedent cases from [relevant courts]
3. Recent developments since [date]

Present findings as:

- Summary of governing law (1-2 paragraphs)
- Analysis of key authorities (bulleted list with brief explanations)
- Potential arguments for both sides
- Conclusion based on current legal landscape

Include citations in [Bluebook/other citation format] style."

16.3   Medical and Healthcare Prompt Engineering

Medical prompting requires scientific accuracy, appropriate caution, and sensitivity to patient care considerations.

Key Considerations for Medical Prompting

1. **Terminology Precision**

   - Use proper medical terminology and classification systems
   - Distinguish between symptoms, signs, diagnoses, and treatments

2. **Evidence-Based Approach**

   - Request information based on current clinical guidelines
   - Specify level of evidence required (e.g., randomized controlled trials)

3. **Patient-Specific Factors**

   - Include relevant demographic and clinical information
   - Consider comorbidities and contraindications

4. **Ethical and Liability Considerations**

   - Include appropriate disclaimers about not replacing professional medical advice
   - Maintain focus on educational content rather than specific treatment recommendations

Example: Clinical Case Analysis Prompt

 Basic Medical Prompt:

"What could cause chest pain?"

Optimized Medical Prompt:

"You are a medical education assistant helping a medical student prepare for clinical rotations. Provide a differential diagnosis for a 58-year-old male patient presenting with acute onset substernal chest pain, radiating to the left arm, associated with shortness of breath and diaphoresis. The patient has a history of hypertension, hyperlipidemia, and type 2 diabetes.

For each potential diagnosis:

1. List key clinical features that support this diagnosis
2. Suggest appropriate initial diagnostic tests
3. Outline first-line management approaches
4. Note red flags that would require immediate intervention

Organize information in order of clinical priority (most urgent/ life-threatening to least). Reference current clinical guidelines where relevant. Include a reminder that this information is for educational purposes and real patients require individualized assessment by qualified healthcare providers."

Medical Literature Review Template

 Template:

"Summarize the current evidence regarding [treatment/ intervention] for [condition] based on medical literature published since [year]. Include:

1. Mechanism of action
2. Efficacy data from key clinical trials
3. Safety profile and common adverse effects
4. Current guideline recommendations
5. Ongoing areas of research or controversy

Present information at a level appropriate for [healthcare professionals/patients/students] with citations to primary literature where possible."

16.4   Financial and Business Prompt Engineering

Financial prompting requires numerical precision, market awareness, and appropriate risk disclosures.

Key Considerations for Financial Prompting

1. **Data Recency and Relevance**

   - Specify time periods for financial analysis
   - Acknowledge limitations of historical data for predictions

2. **Quantitative Precision**

   - Request specific metrics and ratios
   - Specify calculation methodologies

3. **Risk and Uncertainty**

   - Include balanced discussion of upside and downside scenarios
   - Request appropriate risk disclosures

4. **Regulatory Compliance**

   - Incorporate relevant financial regulations
   - Include necessary disclaimers about investment advice

Example: Investment Analysis Prompt

📝 Basic Financial Prompt:

"Analyse this company as an investment."

📝 Optimized Financial Prompt:

"You are a financial analyst assistant preparing an investment report on [Company Name]. Create a comprehensive analysis including:

1. Business Model Assessment

   - Core revenue streams and business units
   - Competitive positioning in the industry
   - Key growth drivers and challenges

2. Financial Performance

- 3-year trend analysis of revenue, EBITDA, and net income
- Key financial ratios (P/E, EV/EBITDA, Debt/Equity)
- Cash flow sustainability and capital allocation strategy

3. Risk Assessment

- Macroeconomic sensitivities
- Industry-specific challenges
- Company-specific risks

4. Valuation Perspective

- Current valuation relative to industry peers
- Potential catalysts for valuation change
- Bull, base, and bear case scenarios

Format as a structured report with executive summary. Include standard disclaimers that this analysis does not constitute investment advice and that all investments carry risk of loss."

Financial Forecasting Template

 Template:

"Develop a 3-year financial forecast model for [business type] based on the following assumptions:

- Annual revenue growth: [percentage range]
- Gross margin: [percentage]
- Operating expense growth: [percentage]
- Tax rate: [percentage]
- Capital expenditure: [amount or percentage of revenue]

Present results in a structured format showing:

1. Income statement projections (annual)
2. Cash flow projections (annual)

3. Key financial ratios for each year
4. Sensitivity analysis for [key variables]

Include notes on methodology and limitations of the forecast."

16.5   Technical and Engineering Prompt Engineering

Technical prompting requires precision, structured problem-solving approaches, and domain-specific knowledge.

Key Considerations for Technical Prompting

1. **Specification Clarity**

   - Define technical requirements precisely
   - Specify relevant standards and protocols

2. **System Context**

   - Provide information about the technical environment
   - Specify constraints and dependencies

3. **Methodology Guidance**

   - Request specific problem-solving approaches
   - Include error handling considerations

4. **Documentation Requirements**

   - Specify code commenting standards
   - Request explanations of technical decisions

Example: Software Development Prompt

📝 Basic Technical Prompt:

"Write code to sort a list."

📝 Optimized Technical Prompt:

"Write a Python function that implements the quicksort algorithm to sort a list of integers. The function should:

1. Handle edge cases (empty lists, single-item lists)
2. Use in-place sorting to minimize memory usage
3. Include time and space complexity analysis in comments
4. Follow PEP 8 style guidelines
5. Include docstrings and type hints
6. Provide example usage

Explain your implementation choices, particularly the pivot selection strategy and its impact on performance with different input distributions."

Technical Documentation Template

 Template:

"Create comprehensive API documentation for a [language] function/method that [function purpose]. Include:

1. Function signature with parameter types and return values
2. Purpose and usage context
3. Parameter descriptions with valid ranges/formats
4. Return value explanation
5. Exception/error handling details
6. Performance characteristics (time/space complexity)
7. Usage examples covering common scenarios
8. Notes on limitations or edge cases

Format the documentation following [standard] conventions."

16.6 Creative and Entertainment Prompt Engineering

Creative fields require different prompting approaches that balance technical guidance with artistic freedom.

Key Considerations for Creative Prompting

1. **Stylistic Guidance**

   - Reference specific genres, artists, or works
   - Define the emotional tone and impact

2. **Structural Elements**

   - Specify format requirements (length, structure)
   - Define key narrative or compositional elements

3. **Audience Considerations**

   - Identify target audience demographics
   - Specify appropriate content restrictions

4. **Creative Constraints**

   - Provide productive limitations that spark creativity
   - Balance guidance with room for AI innovation

Example: Screenwriting Prompt

 Basic Creative Prompt:

"Write a scene about two friends."

 Optimized Creative Prompt:

"Write a 2-page screenplay scene between two former best friends who haven't spoken in five years, now reuniting at an airport. The scene should:

1. Begin with awkward tension but end with a hint of reconciliation
2. Include subtext that reveals their falling out involved a romantic betrayal
3. Use minimal dialogue, emphasizing visual storytelling and body language
4. Take place in a crowded international terminal during a flight delay

5. Follow standard screenplay format with proper scene headings and action descriptions

The tone should balance melancholy with subtle humour, similar to the style of Noah Baumbach films. Target audience is adults 25-40 who enjoy character-driven indie dramas."

Creative Content Brief Template

 Template:

"Create a [content type] about [subject] in the style of [reference]. The piece should:

1. Target [audience demographic] with appropriate tone and complexity
2. Evoke [emotional response] through [stylistic techniques]
3. Include [specific elements or themes]
4. Avoid [problematic content or clichés]
5. Follow [structural format] with approximately [length]

Reference works include [examples] for tone and style guidance."

16.7 Educational and Academic Prompt Engineering

Educational prompting requires pedagogical awareness, accuracy, and adaptation to different learning levels.

Key Considerations for Educational Prompting

1. **Learning Level Specification**

    - Define the target educational level precisely
    - Consider prior knowledge assumptions

2. **Pedagogical Approach**

    - Specify teaching methodologies (inquiry-based, direct instruction)
    - Include scaffolding for complex concepts

3. **Assessment Integration**

   - Request formative checks for understanding
   - Include summative assessment components

4. **Multimodal Learning Support**

   - Incorporate visual, textual, and interactive elements
   - Support different learning styles

Example: Lesson Plan Prompt

 Basic Educational Prompt:

"Create a lesson about photosynthesis."

Optimized Educational Prompt:

"Design a comprehensive 45-minute middle school (7th grade) science lesson plan on photosynthesis that follows the 5E instructional model (Engage, Explore, Explain, Elaborate, Evaluate). The lesson should:

1. Begin with an engaging demonstration or question that activates prior knowledge
2. Include a hands-on experiment using readily available classroom materials
3. Explain the chemical process using age-appropriate language and analogies
4. Connect the concept to climate change and plant ecology
5. Incorporate formative assessment through strategic questioning
6. End with a creative assessment task that demonstrates understanding

Include specific time allocations for each section, required materials, potential misconceptions to address, differentiation strategies for diverse learners, and alignment with Next Generation Science Standards (specifically MS-LS1-6)."

Educational Assessment Template

 Template:

"Create a [formative/summative] assessment for [subject] at the [educational level] that evaluates understanding of [specific concepts]. The assessment should:

1. Include a variety of question types (multiple-choice, short answer, extended response)
2. Assess different cognitive levels according to Bloom's Taxonomy
3. Provide clear scoring criteria or rubrics
4. Include accommodations for diverse learners
5. Align with [specific educational standards]

Provide an answer key with explanations for correct responses."

16.8   Data Science and Analytics Prompt Engineering

Data analysis prompts require statistical rigor, methodological clarity, and visualization guidance.

Key Considerations for Data Science Prompting

1. **Data Context**

   - Specify data sources, formats, and limitations
   - Define relevant variables and their relationships

2. **Analytical Approach**

   - Request specific statistical methods
   - Define confidence levels and significance thresholds

3. **Visualization Requirements**

   - Specify chart types and design elements
   - Define audience and purpose of visualizations

4. **Interpretation Guidance**

- Request business implications of findings
- Specify level of technical detail in explanations

Example: Data Analysis Prompt

📝 Basic Data Science Prompt:

"Analyze this customer dataset."

📝 Optimized Data Science Prompt:

"Perform a comprehensive customer segmentation analysis on this e-commerce transaction dataset containing 10,000 records with the following variables: customer_id, purchase_date, product_category, purchase_amount, customer_age, and customer_location.

1. Begin with exploratory data analysis including summary statistics and distribution visualizations
2. Identify and handle missing values and outliers, explaining your methodology
3. Perform RFM (Recency, Frequency, Monetary) analysis to segment customers
4. Apply k-means clustering (test k=3 to k=7) and determine optimal cluster count using the elbow method
5. Create visualizations showing cluster characteristics using appropriate chart types
6. Provide business interpretations of each segment with actionable marketing recommendations
7. Suggest metrics to track segment performance over time

Present results in a format suitable for both technical data scientists (including methodology details) and business stakeholders (focusing on insights and recommendations)."

Data Visualization Template

 Template:

"Create [visualization type] to represent [data relationship] for [audience]. The visualization should:

1. Clearly show the relationship between [variables]
2. Use appropriate colour schemes for data type (sequential, diverging, or categorical)
3. Include proper labels, legend, and title
4. Avoid chart junk and maintain appropriate data-ink ratio
5. Be accessible (colourblind-friendly, clear contrast)

Provide a brief interpretation of key insights from the visualization."

16.9   Cross-Domain Applications

Many real-world scenarios require combining domain expertise from multiple fields.

Example: Healthcare Marketing Prompt

 Cross-Domain Prompt:

"Develop a comprehensive marketing strategy for a new telemedicine platform specializing in mental health services. The strategy should:

1. Incorporate medical ethics and healthcare privacy regulations (HIPAA)
2. Use evidence-based language about mental health conditions and treatments
3. Apply marketing principles for healthcare services, including appropriate messaging

4. Consider technical aspects of the telemedicine platform in promotional materials
5. Address financial considerations including insurance coverage and pricing models

The target audience is adults 25-45 with employer-provided health insurance. Include recommendations for digital marketing channels, content strategy, and success metrics that respect both healthcare regulations and marketing best practices."

Example: Legal-Technical Documentation Prompt

 Cross-Domain Prompt:

"Create a user agreement for a mobile banking application that balances legal requirements with user experience. The document should:

1. Include all necessary legal protections regarding financial data security
2. Comply with relevant banking regulations and data protection laws
3. Explain technical security features in user-friendly language
4. Structure information in a clear, navigable format
5. Use plain language principles while maintaining legal validity

The document should be suitable for implementation in the US market and include appropriate clauses for data collection, third-party integrations, liability limitations, and dispute resolution."

16.10   Hands-On Exercises: Domain-Specific Prompting

Exercise 1:

Create a medical prompt for generating patient education materials about diabetes management that balances clinical accuracy with accessibility for patients with limited health literacy.

✏️ Exercise 2:

Design a legal prompt for analyzing a commercial lease agreement, identifying potential risks, and suggesting negotiation points.

✏️ Exercise 3:

Develop a technical prompt for creating API documentation for a payment processing system that serves both developers and business stakeholders.

16.11   Summary & Key Takeaways

✔️ Domain-specific prompting requires understanding the unique terminology, standards, and requirements of each field.

✔️ Legal prompts must emphasize jurisdiction, authority, and precise language.

✔️ Medical prompts require scientific accuracy, evidence-based approaches, and appropriate disclaimers.

✔️ Financial prompts need quantitative precision, risk awareness, and regulatory compliance.

✔️ Technical prompts should specify methodologies, system contexts, and documentation standards.

✔️ Creative prompts balance guidance with artistic freedom while defining audience and style.

✔️ Educational prompts incorporate pedagogical approaches and learning level adaptations.

✔️ Cross-domain applications combine expertise from multiple fields for complex scenarios.

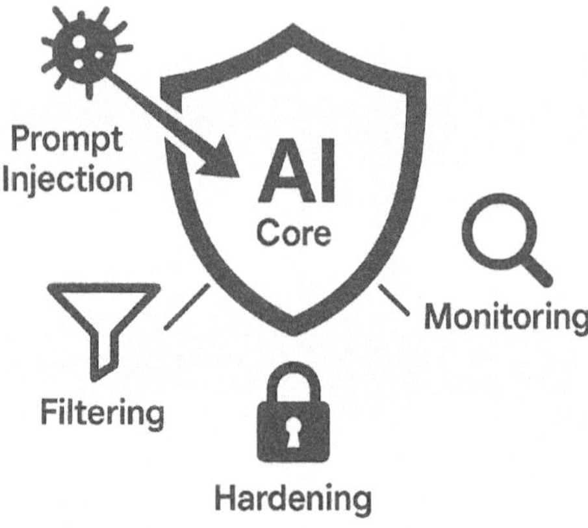

Figure 16.1: Prompt Injection Attacks

🚀 What's Next?

In the next chapter, we'll explore how to build and manage AI agents – autonomous systems that can perform complex tasks through sophisticated prompt engineering.

Building and Managing AI Agents

17.1   Introduction

AI agents represent the next evolution in prompt engineering – autonomous systems that can perform complex tasks with minimal human supervision. Unlike simple prompt-response interactions, AI agents maintain context, make decisions, and execute multi-step processes to achieve specific goals.

This chapter explores how to design, build, and manage AI agents using advanced prompt engineering techniques, enabling more sophisticated AI applications across industries.

Why AI Agents Matter

Traditional prompt engineering focuses on single interactions, but AI agents can:

- Maintain persistent memory across multiple interactions
- Break complex tasks into manageable steps
- Make decisions based on contextual information
- Learn from past interactions to improve performance
- Operate autonomously with appropriate guardrails

17.2   Understanding AI Agent Architecture

AI agents combine several key components to create autonomous systems capable of complex tasks.

Core Components of AI Agents

1. **Memory Systems**

   - Short-term context (current conversation)
   - Long-term storage (persistent knowledge)
   - Episodic memory (past interactions)

2. **Planning Modules**

   - Goal decomposition (breaking tasks into steps)
   - Strategy formulation (determining approach)
   - Error handling and recovery

3. **Tool Integration**

   - API connections to external services
   - Data retrieval capabilities
   - Action execution mechanisms

4. **Self-Monitoring**

   - Progress tracking toward goals
   - Quality assessment of outputs
   - Detection of errors or limitations

Example: Basic AI Agent Architecture

 Example:

User Request → Planning Module → Memory Retrieval → Tool Selection → Action Execution → Response Generation → Self-Evaluation → Refinement Loop

17.3   Designing AI Agents with Advanced Prompt Engineering

Creating effective AI agents requires sophisticated prompt engineering techniques that go beyond single-interaction prompts.

1. Goal-Oriented Prompting

Design prompts that define clear objectives for the AI agent to achieve.

 Prompt:

"You are an AI research assistant. Your goal is to produce a comprehensive literature review on the topic of quantum computing. Break this task into steps, execute each step, and compile the results into a structured report."

✅ Why It Works:

- Provides a clear end goal
- Encourages the AI to plan and structure its approach

2. Context Retention Prompts

Create prompts that instruct the AI to maintain and utilize context over multiple interactions.

 Prompt:

"As you perform this task, maintain a summary of key information discovered. Refer back to this summary in subsequent steps to avoid redundancy and ensure coherence in your final output."

✅ Why It Works:

- Simulates short-term memory
- Improves consistency across multiple interactions

3. Decision-Making Prompts

Design prompts that guide the AI through decision-making processes.

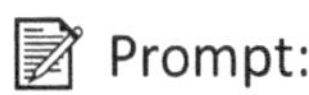 Prompt:

"When faced with multiple research directions, evaluate each option based on relevance to the main topic, availability of recent studies, and potential impact. Choose the most promising direction and explain your reasoning."

 Why It Works:

- Encourages critical thinking
- Provides a framework for making choices

4. Error Handling and Recovery Prompts

Include instructions for dealing with potential issues or limitations.

📝 Prompt:

"If you encounter conflicting information or gaps in your knowledge, acknowledge these limitations in your report. Suggest potential ways to resolve these issues, such as additional research areas or expert consultation."

 Why It Works:

- Improves the robustness of the AI agent
- Encourages transparency about limitations

17.4 Implementing AI Agents with Tool Integration

AI agents become more powerful when they can interact with external tools and APIs. Here's how to design prompts that enable effective tool use.

1. Tool Selection Prompts

Guide the AI in choosing appropriate tools for specific tasks.

📝 Prompt:

"You have access to the following tools: web search API, academic database, and a citation generator. For each step in your research process, select the most appropriate tool and explain why you chose it."

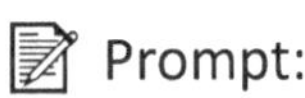 Why It Works:

- Encourages thoughtful tool selection
- Improves efficiency by using the right tool for each task

2. API Interaction Prompts

Provide instructions for how the AI should interact with external APIs.

 Prompt:

"When using the web search API, formulate specific search queries based on your current research question. Analyze the top 5 results and summarize relevant information. If the results are insufficient, refine your query and try again."

Why It Works:

- Guides the AI through the process of using external tools
- Encourages iterative refinement for better results

3. Data Integration Prompts

Instruct the AI on how to incorporate external data into its reasoning and outputs.

Prompt:

"After retrieving information from the academic database, integrate this new data with your existing knowledge. Identify any conflicts or synergies between the new information and what you've already compiled. Update your summary accordingly."

Why It Works:

- Ensures cohesive integration of new information
- Promotes critical analysis of multiple sources

17.5   Managing AI Agent Behaviour

Effective AI agents require careful management to ensure they operate within desired parameters.

1. Ethical Constraint Prompts

Incorporate ethical guidelines into the AI agent's decision-making process.

 Prompt:

"In all your actions, prioritize academic integrity. Do not engage in plagiarism, always cite sources properly, and maintain objectivity in your analysis. If you're unsure about the ethical implications of an action, err on the side of caution and seek clarification."

✅ Why It Works:

- Embeds ethical considerations into the AI's behavior
- Reduces the risk of unintended negative consequences

2. Scope Limitation Prompts

Define clear boundaries for the AI agent's activities.

📌 Example:

📝 Prompt:

"Focus your research exclusively on peer-reviewed articles published in the last five years. Do not include or act on information from social media, blogs, or non-academic sources."

✅ Why It Works:

- Prevents the AI from going off-track
- Ensures the quality and relevance of the agent's output

3. Progress Reporting Prompts

Instruct the AI to provide regular updates on its progress.

 Prompt:

"After completing each major step in your research process, provide a brief progress report. Include what you've accomplished, any challenges encountered, and your next planned actions."

✅ Why It Works:

- Enables monitoring of the AI agent's activities
- Allows for timely intervention if needed

17.6   Evaluating and Improving AI Agent Performance

Continuous evaluation and refinement are crucial for maintaining effective AI agents.

1. Self-Evaluation Prompts

Encourage the AI to assess its own performance and outputs.

 Prompt:

"Once you've completed the literature review, evaluate your work based on comprehensiveness, relevance, and clarity. Identify areas where your analysis could be strengthened or expanded."

✅ Why It Works:

- Promotes continuous improvement
- Helps identify areas for refinement

2. Feedback Integration Prompts

Design prompts that allow the AI to incorporate external feedback.

 Prompt:

"I will provide feedback on your literature review. Analyze this feedback, identify key areas for improvement, and describe how you would modify your approach in future tasks based on this input."

✅ Why It Works:

- Enables the AI to learn from past performance
- Improves the quality of future outputs

3. Comparative Analysis Prompts

Instruct the AI to compare its performance against benchmarks or alternatives.

📌 Example:

📝 Prompt:

"Compare your literature review to this example of a high-quality review in a similar field. Identify differences in structure, depth of analysis, and presentation. What can you learn from this comparison to improve your own work?"

✅ Why It Works:

- Provides concrete examples for improvement
- Encourages critical analysis of different approaches

17.7 Case Studies: AI Agents in Action

Case Study 1: AI Research Assistant

📌 Scenario:

A team of scientists uses an AI agent to assist with literature reviews for cutting-edge quantum computing research.

📌 Key Prompts Used:

1. Goal-setting: "Conduct a comprehensive literature review on topological quantum computing advancements in the last 2 years."
2. Tool integration: "Use the arXiv API to retrieve relevant papers, then summarize key findings."
3. Analysis: "Identify common themes, contradictions, and gaps in the current research landscape."

📌 Results:

- 80% reduction in time spent on initial literature reviews
- Identification of three previously overlooked research opportunities

Case Study 2: AI Project Manager

📌 Scenario:

A software development company deploys an AI agent to assist in project management and task allocation.

📌 Key Prompts Used:

1. Planning: "Break down this software project into main components and suggest a timeline for each."
2. Resource allocation: "Based on team members' skills and current workload, recommend task assignments."
3. Risk assessment: "Analyze the project plan and identify potential bottlenecks or risks."

📌 Results:

- 30% improvement in project completion times
- More balanced workload distribution among team members

Case Study 3: AI Financial Analyst

📌 Scenario:

An investment firm uses an AI agent to assist in market analysis and stock recommendations.

📌 Key Prompts Used:

1. Data gathering: "Collect financial data for the top 100 tech companies from reliable financial APIs."
2. Analysis: "Perform a comparative analysis of these companies based on key financial metrics."
3. Recommendation: "Based on your analysis, suggest the top 5 companies for potential investment, with reasoning."

📌 Results:

- More comprehensive market analysis covering a broader range of factors
- 20% improvement in investment return compared to traditional analysis methods

17.8 Challenges and Future Directions

While AI agents offer tremendous potential, several challenges remain:

1. **Ethical Considerations**: Ensuring AI agents make ethical decisions and respect privacy.
2. **Transparency**: Making the decision-making process of AI agents more interpretable.
3. **Scalability**: Managing the computational resources required for complex AI agents.
4. **Interoperability**: Enabling AI agents to work seamlessly with various tools and platforms.

Future research in AI agent development will likely focus on:

- More sophisticated planning and reasoning capabilities
- Enhanced natural language understanding for better human-AI collaboration
- Improved self-learning mechanisms for continuous performance improvement

17.9 Hands-On Exercise: Design Your Own AI Agent

 **Exercise:**

Design an AI agent to assist in content creation for a digital marketing agency. Include prompts for:

1. Understanding the client's brand and target audience
2. Researching trending topics in the client's industry
3. Generating content ideas and outlines
4. Creating and refining content pieces
5. Analyzing content performance and suggesting improvements

17.10 Summary & Key Takeaways

✔ AI agents represent a significant advancement in AI applications, enabling autonomous, multi-step task completion.

✔ Effective AI agents require sophisticated prompt engineering that covers goal-setting, context retention, decision-making, and error handling.

✔ Tool integration and API interactions expand the capabilities of AI agents.

✔ Managing AI agent behavior through ethical constraints and scope limitations is crucial.

✔ Continuous evaluation and improvement processes are essential for maintaining effective AI agents.

✔ Real-world applications of AI agents show promising results in research, project management, and financial analysis.

✔ Future developments in AI agents will focus on ethical considerations, transparency, scalability, and enhanced reasoning capabilities.

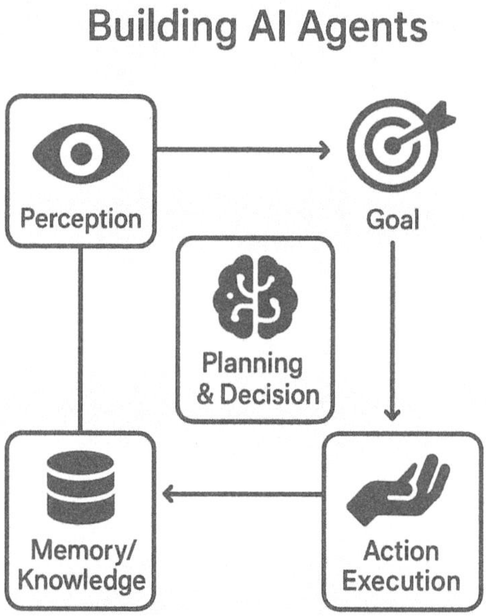

Figure 17.1: Building AI agents

🚀 What's Next?

As AI agent technology continues to evolve, it will open up new possibilities for automation, decision support, and human-AI collaboration across various industries. Staying updated with the latest developments in AI agent design and prompt engineering will be crucial for leveraging these powerful tools effectively.

Summary (It is Not End; It is the New Beginning!!!)

Your quest into the heart of AI communication began the moment you opened this book, stepping from simply *using* AI to truly *understanding* the intricate dialogue required to unlock its vast potential (Chapters 1-2). You learned the fundamental language, the very anatomy of a powerful instruction, laying the groundwork for the mastery to come.

Armed with these essentials, you delved deeper, mastering the 'spells' of advanced prompt engineering – Chain-of-Thought reasoning, nuanced role-playing, and the subtle art of few-shot learning (Chapter 3). Like a skilled artisan learning their tools, you discovered how to adapt your craft, tailoring prompts for the unique minds of different AI models like GPT-4, Claude, and Gemini, shaping their strengths for specific tasks and industries (Chapter 4).

With sharpened skills, you emerged as a digital alchemist, capable of conjuring creative wonders – weaving tales, generating stunning visuals, and composing novel melodies (Chapter 5). You then applied this magic to the practical realm, architecting automated workflows that streamline complex business processes across support, marketing, HR, and finance, transforming manual effort into seamless efficiency (Chapter 6).

But true mastery demands wisdom. Your journey guided you through the critical ethical labyrinth, teaching you to wield AI responsibly, mitigate bias, and champion fairness (Chapter 7). You honed your precision, mastering the art of performance measurement to ensure your AI creations were not just powerful, but consistently accurate and reliable (Chapter 8).

Gazing into the crystal ball of AI's future, you glimpsed the exciting horizon: context-aware systems, autonomous agents like AutoGPT, and the nascent magic of multimodal interactions (Chapter 9). This vision was grounded firmly in reality as you explored real-world adventures where these techniques drive innovation (Chapter 10) and gathered your essential 'wizard's toolkit' of platforms, resources, and communities (Chapter 11).

This quest through *Mastering Prompt Engineering* has equipped you with profound capabilities. You are no longer just interacting with AI; you are a partner in its potential, capable of guiding, shaping, and creating with unprecedented power. The journey doesn't end here; the landscape of AI is ever evolving. Continue to experiment, continue to learn, and continue your adventure, architecting the future of human-AI collaboration (Chapter 12).

The final ascent elevated your craft to true artistry. You learned to **architect the very soul of enterprise AI**, crafting foundational system prompts that define an AI's identity, knowledge, and behaviour within complex organizations (Chapter 13). You became a maestro, **conducting intricate multi-model orchestras**, chaining specialized AIs together in elegant workflows that tackle problems far beyond the reach of any single mind (Chapter 14). Your command expanded further as you learned to **blend digital realities**, mastering multimodal prompting to converse with AI using a symphony of text, image, audio, and video (Chapter 15). Finally, you honed your expertise, learning to **specialize your craft**, adapting your powerful prompting techniques for the demanding, nuanced requirements of specific domains like law, medicine, and finance (Chapter 16).

Chapter 17 is most important, so read again!

References

1. *Claude* [Large language model]. https://claude.ai
2. AI music generation model]. https://www.aiva.ai/
3. *Gemini* [Large language model]. https://gemini.google.com
4. *Hugging Face* [Platform and community for machine learning]. https://huggingface.co/
5. *LLaMA 3* [Large language model]. https://ai.meta.com/llama/
6. *Midjourney* [Image generation model]. https://www.midjourney.com
7. *ChatGPT* [Large language model]. https://chat.openai.com
8. *DALL·E 3* [Image generation model]. https://openai.com/dall-e-3
9. *Perplexity* [AI conversational search engine]. https://www.perplexity.ai
10. *Pika* [AI video generation model]. https://pika.art/
11. *Runway Gen-2* [AI video generation model]. https://runwayml.com/
12. *Stable Diffusion* [Image generation model]. https://stability.ai/stablediffusion
13. *Suno* [AI music generation model]. https://suno.ai/
14. *Zapier* [Workflow automation platform]. https://zapier.com

www.ingramcontent.com/pod-product-compliance
Lightning Source LLC
Chambersburg PA
CBHW041318120726
48005CB00014B/2046